KING'S COLLEGE LONDON
MEDIEVAL STUDIES

XVIII

King's College London
Centre for Late Antique & Medieval Studies

Director: Janet L. Nelson

KING'S COLLEGE LONDON MEDIEVAL STUDIES

GENERAL EDITOR:
Janet Bately

EXECUTIVE EDITOR:
David Hook

The *Carmina Burana*:
Four Essays

Edited by Martin H. Jones

King's College London
Centre for Late Antique & Medieval Studies
2000

The following texts in this publication are printed with the permission of Art Esprit Ltd:

The World of the *Carmina Burana* (Anne J. Duggan)
Latin Songs in the *Carmina Burana*:
Profane Love and Satire (Peter Dronke)
The German Texts in the *Codex Buranus* (Cyril Edwards)
Earthly Delights: the Pictorial Images of the
Carmina Burana Manuscript (Julia Walworth)

British Library Cataloguing in Publication Data

A catalogue record for this book is available
from the British Library

ISSN 0953-217X
ISBN 0 9539838 0 3

Printed in England on acid-free paper by

Short Run Press Ltd
Exeter
2000

CONTENTS

CONTRIBUTORS

Peter Dronke
Professor of Medieval Latin Literature,
University of Cambridge

Anne J. Duggan
Senior Lecturer in History,
King's College, University of London

Cyril Edwards
formerly Lecturer in German,
University of Oxford

Martin H. Jones
Senior Lecturer in German,
King's College, University of London

Julia Walworth
Head of Historic Collections Service,
University of London Library

PREFACE

The essays in this volume began life as lectures which were delivered at a public symposium held at the Barbican Centre in London on 14 December 1996. The symposium, entitled 'Understanding the *Carmina Burana* Today', was one of a number of events organized to accompany an exhibition which was staged at the Barbican Centre from November 1996 to January 1997 to commemorate the one-hundred-and-fiftieth anniversary of the publication of the first edition of the contents of the *Carmina Burana* manuscript, the *Codex Buranus*, by Andreas Schmeller in 1847. The whole project, encompassing the exhibition, a concert performance of Carl Orff's cantata *Carmina Burana*, a showing of Jean-Pierre Ponnelle's film *Carmina Burana*, and the symposium, was conceived and executed by Art Esprit Ltd. The symposium was arranged in collaboration with the Centre for Late Antique and Medieval Studies of King's College London, on whose behalf the editor of this volume acted as the symposium co-ordinator.

The exhibition included displays about the manuscript of the *Carmina Burana* and illustrated the power of this uniquely rich collection of medieval poetry to inspire creative work in the twentieth century through sections devoted to the life and work of Carl Orff, poems especially composed for the occasion by the Liverpool poet Brian Patten, and a collection of oil paintings, monoprints, and etchings on themes from the *Carmina Burana* commissioned by Art Esprit Ltd. from the Cypriot-born British artist John Kiki.

Within the project as a whole, the specific objectives of the symposium were to provide the stimulus for a reassessment of the *Codex Buranus* and its contents in the light of current scholarship by experts in a variety of fields and to make that reassessment accessible to an audience made up of both specialists and non-specialists in medieval studies. The lectures have been revised for publication principally by the inclusion of references to sources, editions, and scholarly literature and by the addition of some detailed material which was not suitable for the lecture format. Where it was thought helpful, suggestions for further reading have been appended to the essays. The essays thus preserve in large measure the original lecture style and aim to reach non-specialists as well as specialists, but each represents a new and distinctive contribution to the understanding of the *Carmina Burana*.

The volume is opened, as was the symposium, by Anne Duggan's evocative account of the social and intellectual environment in which the contents of the codex were composed. This was above all the student world of the nascent universities in the late twelfth and early thirteenth centuries. Drawn from all corners of Europe, the scholastic populations at the great centres of learning made up lively, sometimes volatile communities, which however enjoyed special privileges as the institutions of Church and secular government competed for their services. The Latin-based education offered at the leading schools of the time gave the educational élite access to a world of opportunity and intellectual exchange which transcended national boundaries. By turns learned, satirical, idealistic, amorous, bawdy, and cynical, the Latin poetry of the *Codex Buranus* reflects the life of the intelligentsia, and particularly its youthful elements, at a time of conspicuous change in educational practices and in society at large.

Peter Dronke focuses in his essay on the Latin songs which constitute the bulk of the collection, demonstrating the diversity of their themes and origins and underlining the status of the *Codex Buranus* as a signal witness of secular lyrical composition in Latin in the twelfth and thirteenth centuries. He chooses for close analysis five songs which exemplify the international nature of the collection as a whole and represent two of its dominant strands, love and satire. The songs examined reveal remarkable variety and, at times, great psychological complexity in the depiction of love. The analyses presented in this essay culminate in the examination of a gem of a song which includes some German verses among the Latin, blends the learned and the folkloristic, and above all evokes a love in which *amor* and *caritas* are so inseparably linked as to present a direct challenge to modern views of medieval thinking about the nature of love.

Although it is essentially a repository of compositions in Latin, the *Codex Buranus* is notable for its admixture of elements in other languages, chief among these being German. In his essay Cyril Edwards surveys the German texts in the manuscript and assesses their importance for the history of medieval German literature. The texts include interlinear glosses in Latin texts, passages of German in Easter and passion plays, a translation of John 1.1-14, examples of lyric genres poorly represented in the later German manuscript collections of songs, and strophes by some of the most famous of the Middle High German *Minnesänger*, appended to Latin lyrics. Through the very diversity of these and other texts in the vernacular, the codex affords valuable insights into the uses of written German in the thirteenth century. An appendix drawn up for the published version of the lecture provides a comprehensive index to the German material in the manuscript.

One of the many mysteries that surround the *Codex Buranus* concerns the question of patronage. At whose behest, at whose expense was the manuscript compiled? The eight miniatures in the manuscript do not in themselves answer this question, but, as Julia Walworth observes in her essay on the pictorial images, their presence indicates the high value that the patron placed on the production of the manuscript. Much that pertains to the illustrations remains the subject of speculation. The individual images can, however, be shown to have analogues in other manuscripts (though not ones devoted to lyrical poetry), with one conspicuous exception, namely the single full-page miniature in the manuscript, which depicts two forest scenes [Pl. 8]. This is without parallel in its time. In its uniqueness and with its exuberant variety of forms, it is, as Julia Walworth suggests in the words which conclude the volume, a fitting pictorial image not only of the songs of springtime which it accompanies, but also of the whole manuscript of the *Carmina Burana*.

For permission to reproduce photographs, the authors and editor wish to thank the following:

the Staatsbibliothek zu Berlin — Preußischer Kulturbesitz,
the Universitätsbibliothek, Erlangen-Nürnberg,
the Forschungsbibliothek, Gotha,
the Universitätsbibliothek, Heidelberg,
Bildarchiv Foto Marburg,
the Bayerische Staatsbibliothek, Munich,
the Bibliothèque nationale de France, Paris,
the Österreichische Nationalbibliothek, Vienna.

The editor also wishes to record thanks to all those who contributed to the success of the symposium in the first place and subsequently to the production of this volume. These include the authors of the essays themselves; Carol Magner, who assisted in the preparation of Professor Dronke's paper for publication; Professor Janet Nelson, Director of the Centre for Late Antique and Medieval Studies, for approving the Centre's collaboration in the project; and the editorial board of King's College London Medieval Studies, and especially its Executive Director, Professor David Hook, for accepting the volume for publication. Above all thanks are due to Linda M. Rabuzin and Ivan Prpić-Vuna of Art Esprit Ltd.: not only did they conceive the idea of the *Carmina Burana* project, including an academic symposium which would give a stimulus to research, but they have also supported the publication of the lectures in this form, assisting in the preparation of camera-ready copy. The inspiration behind the *Carmina Burana* project as a whole was the wish to promote the sense of a common European heritage, for which the *Codex Buranus* stands as an appropriate symbol. It is to be hoped that this volume will play its part in fulfilling that aspiration.

Martin H. Jones

THE WORLD OF THE *CARMINA BURANA*

Anne J. Duggan

The collection of songs and poetry assembled in MS Clm 4660 and 4660a in the Bavarian State Library in Munich, from the Benedictine monastery of Benediktbeuern in Bavaria, is the largest surviving collection of medieval Latin poetry. Although some of the compositions are the product of known and admired twelfth- and early-thirteenth-century poets—the Archpoet of Cologne (*fl.* 1160s), Walter of Châtillon (died *c.* 1204), Peter of Blois (died 1212), and Philip (de Grève) the Chancellor of Paris (died 1236/37)[1]—most are anonymous, and about half are known only in this manuscript. Essentially, therefore, the *Codex Buranus* is a compilation of contemporary or near-contemporary Latin verse, modelled on the collections of classical poetry and prose assembled for school use from the ninth century onwards; but it differs from them by including fifty or so German verses, some by renowned authors like Walther von der Vogelweide (died *c.* 1228),[2] and some combining Latin and German in bilingual compositions.[3] About half are love-songs (*CB* 56-156), ranging from the elevated to the yearning and the frankly bawdy, and the remainder comprise moral-satirical verses (*CB* 1-55: 20%) and drinking and gaming songs (*CB* 187-226: 12%), completed by two short religious dramas (*CB* 227-28) and a supplement of more varied material (*CB* 1a*-26a*: 15%) added in the mid-thirteenth century (*c.* 1230-50).

---

[1] The Archpoet, *CB* 191; Walter of Châtillon, *CB* 3, 8, 41, 123; Peter of Blois, *CB* 29-31, 63, 67, 69, 72, 83-4, 108; Philip the Chancellor, *CB* 21, [?26], 27, 34, 131, 189.
[2] *CB* 151a, 211a.
[3] German: *CB* 48a, 112a, 113a, 114a, 115a, 135a, 136a, 137, 137a, 138a, 139a, 140a, 141a, 142a, 143a, 144a, 145a, 146a, 147a, 148a, 150a, 151a, 152a, 153a, 155a, 161a, 162a, 163a, 164a, 165a, 166a, 167a, 168a, 169a, 170a, 171a, 172a, 173a, 174a, 175a, 178a, 179a, 180a, 181a, 182a, 183a, 203a, 211a, 2*; Latin and German: *CB* 149, 177, 180, 184-5, 204, 218.

The place of compilation has been debated since the first published edition of the manuscript in 1847, but Bernhard Bischoff dated it to *c.* 1230 and located it variously, either in the south of a Bavarian-speaking area (Carinthia or the Tyrol) or in southern Austria, perhaps the household of the bishop of Seckau. It was not a monastic product: script and content point to a clerical-scholarly milieu, and Olive Sayce[4] has suggested Bressanone (Brixen) in the Tyrol, then German-speaking and ruled by German or Italo-German bishops, as the place of compilation of the main text (to fol. 106*v*), although its two principal scribes were Romance speakers, respectively Italian and French.

The essential context of the *Carmina Burana*, then, is the student world of the late twelfth-early thirteenth century, *c.* 1150-1230, when the earliest universities were coming into existence in the wake of a fundamental transformation in the structure and content of higher learning. Until the end of the eleventh century, monastic schools, like that at Bec-Hellouin in Normandy, had formed the core of higher education in the West. From the beginning of the twelfth century, however, there was a shift from abbey to cathedral, from an education aimed at the spiritual and moral formation of the cloistered monk to one increasingly adjusted to the needs of secular clerks destined for public careers of service in Church and state. This transition was paralleled by changes in teaching method, with increasing emphasis on disputation, the progressive reception of Aristotelian logic, and the application of dialectical argument to every branch of study. The *Artes* were being transformed. John of Salisbury, who spent twelve years in the schools in Paris in the mid-twelfth century, acquiring not only mastery of the Latin language but a deep knowledge of the Latin classics, poured scorn on the 'logic-choppers' who were taking over in the schools. In his view, the Arts were being prostituted. Love of learning for its own sake, delight in the Latin fathers and classics, cultivation of the skills of poetry and good style were being relegated in favour of the utilitarian mastery of useful Latin, laced with just

---

[4]   Olive Sayce, *Plurilingualism in the Carmina Burana: a study of the linguistic and literary influences on the Codex*, Göppinger Arbeiten zur Germanistik, 556 (Göppingen: Kümmerle, 1992), pp. 198-203.

enough classical learning to make it respectable. What the chanceries of Europe wanted was not Ciceronian rhetoric but competent, accurate, and reasonably effective Latin composition.

The turn of the twelfth century coincided with the establishment of recording and taxing bureaucracies of every kind. It was at precisely this time, for example, that the impressive runs of English public records began *(Curia Regis Rolls, Close and Patent Rolls, Memoranda Rolls)*. The expansion of the schools (in Auxerre, Bologna, Cologne, Laon, Montpellier, Orléans, Pavia, Paris, Rheims, Salerno, and elsewhere) reflected the need for trained clerks; and the entry of the new learned élite into the curias of kings, bishops, and nobles can be traced in the increasing number of *magistri* who feature in the witness lists of legal, diplomatic, and administrative documents of all kinds. Inception (that is, admission to the gild of Masters) in a recognized school allowed a student to call himself *Magister*, and the title provided a ready entrance to lucrative professions. Then as now good schools ensured good jobs. Even the papal Curia recruited staff from Orléans, then the best regarded school for the teaching of Latin composition.

At the same time, new subjects joined the ancient hierarchy of theology and the *artes* of grammar, rhetoric, and logic: principally the two laws, Roman and canon, and medicine. By the end of the twelfth century, a small number of *studia* had established international reputations for themselves, attracting students from all over Europe: Paris for arts, theology, and law; Bologna and Pavia for law; and Montpellier and Salerno for medicine—the Harvard, Yale, and Princeton of their day.[5] All shared the same characteristics of an

---

[5]   Further *studia generalia* (as distinct from *studia particularia*, cathedral and urban schools which served local needs) emerged at Reggio (1188), Palencia (1208/09), Oxford (beginning of thirteenth century), Cambridge (1205/25), Arezzo (1215), Salamanca (before 1218/19), Padua (1222), Naples (1224: founded by Emperor Frederick II), Vercelli (1228), Toulouse (1229), Orléans (*c.* 1235). Save for the imperial foundation of the university of Naples in 1224, the dates in brackets refer not to the origin of the *studium* but to its recognition as a *studium generale*: see Jacques Verger, 'Patterns', in *A History of the University in Europe*, edited by Walter Rüegg, I, *The Universities in the Middle Ages*, edited by Hilde de Ridder-Symoens (Cambridge: Cambridge University Press), 1992, pp. 35-74, esp. 62-65 and 69 (for dates and map).

international student and teaching body, and their graduates were to be found in the papal Curia and in the courts of kings, bishops, and nobles, from Scandinavia to Sicily and from Portugal to Poland. The universities thus created a 'European Community' of learning, united by a single language (Latin) which transcended national boundaries, with similar teaching methods, courses of study, and books. To go to one of these schools was to enter an intellectual élite; to make friends who would last a lifetime; to join a kind of brotherhood, with links across Europe. The Englishman John of Salisbury's friendship with the later Abbot Peter of St-Rémi in Rheims was formed during their adolescent years in Paris. Such friendship entailed active commitment which could be called in at any moment. In the 1180s, for example, Stephen of Tournai, then abbot of Sainte-Geneviève in Paris, requested the help of the powerful Cardinal Gratian (formerly, Master Gratian of Pisa) in presenting a case at the papal Curia and recalled that they had first met in the law schools in Bologna, some forty years before, when they heard the lectures of the renowned Roman lawyer Bulgarus, first of the 'four doctors'.[6]

Lifelong friendships between young men of different backgrounds were one consequence of education in the schools; entry into lucrative careers outside one's own country was another. Learned Englishmen, for example, made distinguished careers in Continental Europe. Master Gerard Pucelle was master of the cathedral school in Cologne in the 1160s; Master Ralph, from Sarre in Kent, ruled the schools in Rheims, before becoming dean of the metropolitan church; Master John of Salisbury became bishop of Chartres in 1176. In reverse, Master Vacarius, from Bologna, taught Roman Law in Oxford before joining the *familia* of the archbishop of York; Master Peter of Blois (some of whose poems are found in the *Carmina Burana*) served both the archbishop of Canterbury and the English crown, after abandoning Sicily, where he had been tutor to King William II; and Master Simon of Apulia was chancellor and dean of York in the 1190s.

---

[6]   *Patrologiae cursus completus, series latina (Patrologia latina)*, edited by J.P. Migne, 217 vols (Paris: Garnier, 1844-64) *(= PL)*, CCXI, 338 no. 38. Gratian was cardinal deacon of SS. Cosma e Damiano 1178-1206.

The schools were melting-pots; but they were also powerful centres of cross-fertilization between inner and outer Europe, between secular and clerical culture, between town and country. The young men went home filled up with a new learning, new skills, and an arrogance to match the skills.

Not everyone applauded this turn of events. At the end of the century (1192-1203) Bishop Stephen of Tournai (who had earlier exploited his student friendship with Cardinal Gratian) wrote indignantly to the Pope (Celestine III or Innocent III):

> Contrary to the sacred canons there is public disputation as to the incomprehensible deity. [...] The indivisible Trinity is cut up and wrangled over in the trivia, so that now there are as many errors as doctors, as many scandals as classrooms, as many blasphemies as squares. [...] The faculties called liberal having lost their liberty are sunk in such servitude that adolescents with long hair impudently usurp their professorships, and beardless youths sit in the seat of their seniors, and those who don't yet know how to be disciples strive to be named masters.

And he called for reform of the 'disorder in teaching, learning and disputing', 'lest what is holy be given to dogs and pearls be trodden under foot by swine'.[7] The swine, of course, are the hordes of young Arts students, soaking up a superficial mastery of grammar and dialectic, without the long and careful study of the ancients which had characterized the education of earlier generations.

sed retro actis seculis	In days gone by we were required
vix licuit discipulis	to stick with study; none retired
tandem nonagenarium	or wished himself to be released
quiescere post studium.	till ninety years of age at least.*
(Florebat olim studium, CB 6, 9-12)	

---

[7]   *PL,* CCXI, 516-18 no. 251, translated in Lynn Thorndike, *University Records and Life in the Middle Ages* (New York: Columbia University Press, 1944), pp. 24-25.
*   For verse translations so marked, see *Selections from the Carmina Burana: a verse translation*, translated by David Parlett (Harmondsworth: Penguin, 1986; rpt 1988).

But the delight in argument which scandalized the then sober Stephen of Tournai was fun for the clever young men who had the world and its opportunities before them. The university techniques of *lectura* and *quaestiones disputatae*, which emphasized critical examination of texts and a lively discussion of the opinions of different masters, put a premium on quick-wittedness and skilful debate. Abelard had used his dialectical skills to devastating effect against his own master, William of Champeaux, in the early twelfth century, and thereby made his reputation; the young scholars of the late twelfth and early thirteenth century were increasingly schooled in the same clever tricks of logic. As early as 1155-57 John of Salisbury had satirized in verse the new breed of cocky young artists:

> I am a resident of the Petit-Pont, a new authority in Arts,
> As I boast that previous discoveries are my own;
> What the elders taught, but dear youth does not know,
> I swear was the discovery of my own breast;
> A zealous crowd of youth surrounds me and thinks,
> When I make extravagant boasts, that I speak only the truth.[8]

And he confessed that 'with youthful levity' even he had learned 'to account my knowledge more important than it was'.[9] Practical Latin, logic, and law were the new skills of the twelfth century, solvents of the old culture. Much as today's computer-based knowledge-systems put powerful tools into the hands of the young, logic and dialectic gave ready advantage to youthful scholars:

---

[8]   John of Salisbury, *Entheticus de dogmate philosophorum*, edited by Ronald E. Pepin, *Traditio*, XXXI (1975), 127-93, at p. 139 (ll. 49-54); cf. the translation in Thorndike, *University Records*, pp. 14-15.

[9]   John of Salisbury, *Metalogicon* (1159), edited by Clement C. J. Webb (Oxford: Oxford University Press, 1929), II. 10; cf. *The Metalogicon of John of Salisbury: a twelfth-century defense of the verbal and logical arts of the trivium*, translated by Daniel D. McGarry (Berkeley: University of California Press, 1955, rpt 1962), p. 97.

Iam pueris astutia	For students hardly in their prime
contingit ante tempora,	find themselves wise before their time
qui per malivolentiam	they know it all—impertinence
excludunt sapientiam. [...]	replaces plain intelligence. [...]
at nunc decennes pueri	Now lads of barely a decade
decusso iugo liberi	can graduate—get themselves made
se nunc magistros iactitant,	professors too! And who's to mind
ceci cecos precipitant,	how blind the blind who lead the blind?
implumes aves volitant,	So fledglings soar upon the wing
brunelli chordas incitant,	so donkeys play the lute and sing;
boves in aula salitant,	bulls dance about at court like sprites;
stive precones militant.	and ploughboys sally forth as knights.*

(Florebat olim studium, CB 6, 5-8, 13-20)

The first statutes for the new university of Paris, laid down by Robert de Courçon in 1215, were the fruits of such denunciations of the academic free-for-all that had resulted from the rapid and uncontrolled growth in the Parisian schools. He declared that no one might lecture in Arts before the age of twenty—and he must have completed at least six years in the schools; while in 1252 a minimum course of four or five years was required, and 'determination' (that is, graduation to the baccalaureate) might not be before the age of nineteen. Moreover: fashionable dress was forbidden. Masters must wear all-enveloping black cloaks and avoid 'shoes that are ornamented or with elongated pointed toes'![10]

The schools were not hermetically sealed clerical institutions. Colleges were being founded for 'poor students' (like the Collège des Dix-huit in Paris founded in the 1180s by Joscius of London), but most students hired lodgings, just as their masters often had to hire lecture-rooms to teach in. The young men were thus living singly or in groups, financing themselves from parental income, minor benefices, or doing tutoring work and assisting the teaching masters with the drudgery of bread-and-butter lectures. Student life was therefore freer and less constrained than we might imagine; and students enjoyed the privilege

---

[10] Thorndike, *University Records*, pp. 28-29, 53.

of clerical status (although most were merely tonsured or in minor orders), with few of the restraints which would later attach to holding office in the Church. Their association with the clerical order exempted them from the jurisdiction of the local courts, subjecting them only to the discipline of their own Masters and the diocesan bishop. For young men let loose in a thronging city, away from the restrictions of their home environment, the tavern, the gaming-house, and the young women of the town [pls. 10-12] were potent counter-attractions to the rigours of the lecture-room. As the Archpoet of Cologne[11] recorded in his humorous *Confession*:

Quis Papie demorans	Who ensconced in Pavia
castus habeatur,	seeks chaste sojourning
ubi Venus digito	where Venus with come-hither eyes
iuvenes venatur,	and cheeks adorned for rapture
oculis illaqueat,	crooks a finger to secure
facie predatur?	another youthful capture?*
(Estuans intrinsecus, CB 191, 8, 2-4)	

As their numbers grew, the scholarly associations became significant players in the economic life of the city and could use the threat of secession to force the local authorities to accede to their terms. Estimates for Paris suggest that at the end of the twelfth century the scholars constituted about ten per cent of the population of the city (between 2,500 and 5,000 in a population of 25,000-50,000);[12] and most were 'foreign', in the sense that they did not hail from the city:

---

[11] This title denotes his service of Archbishop Rainald of Cologne, not his own national origins, which cannot be more narrowly defined than 'north of the Alps'. I am grateful to Professor Dronke for this clarification.

[12] A.B. Cobban, *The Medieval Universities: their development and organization* (London: Methuen, 1975), p. 79, citing John W. Baldwin, *Masters, Princes, and Merchants: the social views of Peter the Chanter and his circle,* 2 vols (Princeton: Princeton University Press, 1970), I, 72; II, 51 n. 52.

Exul ego clericus	I, a scholar far from home,
ad laborem natus	born of poor relations
tribulor multotiens	suffer every single day,
paupertati datus.	poverty's privations.*
(Exul ego clericus, CB 129, 1)	

In Paris (and elsewhere) the Arts students and masters banded together for mutual protection and so formed associations reflecting their regional origins. It was from these informal groupings that the division of the faculty of Arts into four 'Nations' derived: French, English-German, Norman, and Picard. In Bologna, the foreign law-students formed similar associations, called *universitates* (of which there were four in 1204), which coalesced into the *Ultramontani* and *Citramontani* by the middle years of the thirteenth century. Although they shared the same intellectual ethos, the students did not abandon their regional affiliations or characteristics. 'The English are drunken cowards', wrote Jacques de Vitry, a renowned preacher who had studied Theology at Paris (died 1240):

> the French proud, soft and effeminate, the Germans are quarrelsome and foul-mouthed, the Normans vain and haughty, the men of Poitou treacherous and miserly, the Burgundians stupid brutes, the Bretons frivolous and flighty, the Lombards miserly, spiteful, and evil-minded, the Romans vicious and violent, the Sicilians tyrannical and cruel, the men of Brabant are thieves and the Flemings are debauched.[13]

While it does not provide an accurate characterization of the Parisian students of his time, this not-unbiased view nevertheless confirms both their international character and their unsavoury reputation among the serious-minded.

---

[13] D.C. Munro, *The Medieval Student,* Translations and reprints from the original sources of European history, 2/3 (Philadelphia: Department of History, University of Pennsylvania Press, 1902), pp. 19-20, from Jacques de Vitry, *Historia Occidentalis*, vii: *de statu Parisiensis civitatis*, edited by J. F. Hinnebusch (Fribourg: Fribourg University Press, 1972), p. 92; cf. Hilde de Ridder-Symoens, 'Mobility', in *The Universities in the Middle Ages*, (see n. 5 above), pp. 280-304, at p. 282.

Their numbers, their rootlessness, and their youth made the students obstreperous, yet secular and ecclesiastical authorities vied with one another to encourage and protect them. In Bologna, the single most important privilege was conferred by the emperor Frederick I in 1155. Known as the Authentic *Habita* (because it was an imperial decree *(Authenticum)* beginning *Habita*), it granted imperial protection to laymen travelling to and from the *studium* and legal exemption within the city. It became a kind of *Magna Carta* of student status throughout Europe for the rest of the Middle Ages. In Paris, the first recorded royal charter resulted from a violent town-gown dispute in which a German student, Henry de Jacea, archdeacon and bishop-elect of Liège, led an attack on a tavern-keeper accused of overcharging for wine. Thomas, the royal Provost of Paris, counter-attacked the German hostel, killing some of the students. The Masters threatened to close the schools and leave the city, unless the king punished the malefactors.[14] The result was the grant of King Philip II's great charter of student privilege, which gave royal protection to the scholars and obliged the citizens by oath to observe its regulations. *Parens scientiarum*, the papal privilege bestowed by Pope Gregory IX in 1231,[15] was similarly the consequence of a violent quarrel over the price of wine, in the bourg-St.-Marcel. Outfaced on the day, the students armed themselves with clubs and swords, wrecked the tavern and rioted through the *quartier*, attacking any who stood in their way. Again, the authorities over-reacted; students were attacked indiscriminately and several were killed. In retaliation, the Masters not only suspended lectures but dispersed the University (Oxford and Cambridge benefited from this dispersion). This time it took two years of negotiations and the papal privilege reinforcing the status of the scholars to induce the Masters to return to the city!

Paris was the New Athens. Just as the empire had been translated from the East to the West, from the Greeks to the Romans, in a *translatio imperii* in 800,[16] so had learning in a corresponding *translatio studii*

---

[14] Stephen C. Ferruolo, '*Parisius-Paradisus*: The City, Its Schools, and the Origins of the University of Paris', in *The University and the City*, edited by Thomas Bender (Oxford: Oxford University Press, 1988), pp. 22-43, at p. 31.

[15] Thorndike, *University Records*, pp. 35-39.

[16] Ferruolo, '*Parisius-Paradisus*', p. 33.

been translated from Egypt to Greece, to Rome, and finally to Paris, that 'mother of sciences', as the papal privilege called it. 'Neither Athens nor Egypt ever had as many scholars as Paris now does', wrote William the Breton in 1210.

The students formed a highly privileged and visible section of society, protected by king, pope, and emperor, who all used their services, masters and students moving freely from school to school as opportunity and advantage took them. So the *Carmina Burana* reflect a youth culture—a privileged, ambitious, self-confident youth culture, which crossed social and political barriers, upwardly and geographically mobile. The collection is full of that excitement, that daring, that laughing-at-convention which characterizes independently minded youth.

> quod prior etas respuit   Ideas our parents used to shun
> iam nunc latius claruit: shine in the eyes of everyone:
> iam calidum in frigidum   what's moist is now called dry, and what
> et humidum in aridum.   once passed for cold now counts as hot.*
> *(Florebat olim studium, CB 6, 37-40)*

The *Carmina Burana* grew from a Latin-based culture; but it was Latin of a peculiar kind. Latin was not the vernacular tongue of any region. Although it was the language of the Church, the schools, the canon and civil law, and most secular administrations, it was no one's mother tongue; no one learned it at his mother's knee or from his nurse; it was an acquired *lingua franca* which had to be learned in early youth, often with the assistance of the rod! Utilitarian as the teaching was, it nevertheless emphasized the memorization of excerpts from the great classical poets and encouraged imitative composition. Poetry was not a frivolous pursuit. Bernard of Chartres (died *c.* 1130), credited with introducing good teaching practices into the cathedral school at Chartres, had encouraged young boys to learn and imitate antique poets as a means of mastering the language. He explained the style of the 'poets and orators who were to serve as models for the boys [...] in imitating prose and poetry', and he made them 'compose prose and poetry every day, and exercise their faculties in discourses between themselves'.[17] Even though Bernard's high standards were not maintained, poetical composition remained intrinsic to the learning of Latin throughout the twelfth century, and an ability to compose Latin verse was a measure of excellence. This was the milieu which produced and popularized the *Carmina Burana*: the play on the genitive, dative, and ablative cases of the Latin noun in the last verse of *Manus ferens munera*, the partial conjugation of the verb 'to give' in the third verse of *Ecce torpet probitas*, and the opening of *Lude, ludat, ludite* echo the declination practice to which novice Latinists were subjected.[18]

Once mastered, however, good Latin enabled entry into an international network which made for ready movement to and from the courts of Europe: royal, episcopal, papal, and aristocratic. Some moralists questioned whether it was proper for a cleric to engage in secular administration; but most accepted such service as a natural part of life—and as a means of rapid advancement. Yet the tensions between the two paths—clerical service of the church and clerical service of the lay establishment—is evident in the *Carmina Burana*, where venality and patronage are the chief targets of the satirists. The quickest way to a bishopric in most parts of Europe was probably royal, not ecclesiastical, service; and successful royal service meant the cultivation of the arts of courtship: flattery, intrigue, and the use of influence. Talent could indeed make its way up the ladder, but it needed recognition, employment, and assistance.

The youths who wrote or sang or listened to the *Carmina Burana* were at the beginning of uncertain careers. They saw the way of the world in stark and vibrant colours, by turns elevated, critical, satirical, and bawdy. Many of the compositions reveal a boyish delight in mastering the necessary Latin, without which entry into the professions was impossible; they show also the preoccupations of youth. More than half are love poetry: whether real or ideal is a matter for debate.

---

[17] As recorded in John of Salisbury's *Metalogicon*, I. 24; cf. *The Metalogicon of John of Salisbury*, translated by McGarry (see n. 9 above), pp. 68-70.
[18] *CB* 1,6, 7-10: 'ablativos [...] dativos [...] genitivos'; *CB* 3,3,2: 'do das dedi dare'; *CB* 172,1,1. Cf. *CB* 5 and 20.

The bi- and multilingualism, combining elements of German, Italian, French, Provençal (and even a little Greek) with Latin, places them at the interface between the learned and the unlearned, with influences passing in both directions, but they are predominantly Latin and reflect the cultivated culture of the schools.

That culture drew on ancient roots. The young 'artists' had learned their Latin by copying the style of the ancients: by reading not only extracts from Virgil and Horace, and Cato's sound sayings, but Ovid's *Ars Amatoria*, Juvenal's *Satires*, and Terence's frank and bawdy *Comedies*. Theirs was a world which defined itself by its specialist learning, and it displayed its distinctive erudition in verses filled with echoes of and allusions to the classical and Christian foundations of its culture. The ideas of classical authors, more or less understood according to the amount of time devoted to them in a particular course of study, were interwoven with those of the Church Fathers, the Old and New Testament, and the contemporary ideals and images of courtly love. The result was a heady mix of reference and metaphor, embracing Ovid, Andreas Capellanus, and Solomon's Song of Songs, in which the goddess Venus could be assimilated to the Virgin Mary, and Blanchefleur, heroine of the medieval romance *Floire et Blancheflor* (*c.* 1167), could be invoked beside Helen of Troy:

Ave, formosissima,	Greetings, most beautiful one,
gemma pretiosa,	precious jewel!
ave, decus virginum,	Greetings, glory of maidens,
virgo gloriosa,	maiden of fair fame!
ave, lumen luminum,	Greetings, light of lights!
ave, mundi rosa,	Greetings, rose of the world,
Blanziflŏr et Helena,	a Blanchefleur, a Helen,
Venus generosa!	a noble Venus![19]
(Si linguis angelicis: CB 77, 8)	

---

[19] This translation is from *Love Lyrics from the Carmina Burana*, edited and translated by P.G. Walsh (Chapel Hill: University of North Carolina Press, 1993), p. 62, whose excellent annotations (pp. 68-73) explain the extraordinary range of the allusions in the poem; cf. Parlett's version in *Selections from the Carmina Burana*, p. 85.

Just as the schools were being transformed by new learning and new pressures, the Church was undergoing rapid development. From struggles with the empire the papacy was emerging as an international authority, presiding at general councils and issuing general decrees. Its central bureaucracy was becoming a civil service open to all the talents, and its legal status was being defined. By the end of the twelfth century that papacy was a central court of appeal to which cases could be referred by any litigant, and through rapid development following the compilation of Gratian's *Decretum (c.* 1140-41), canon law became one of the learned laws, modelled on Roman legal processes and taking its place as an academic study with the *codex iuris civilis* issued by the sixth-century Emperor Justinian. Central to this development was the practice of papal judges delegate and the issue of papal rescripts, called decretal letters, which responded to appeals and answered consultations on points of law or procedure. Collected from the middle years of the century, by the 1190s there were substantial *compendia* of recent law, drawn up for the guidance of local judges, which would in 1234 be compiled into an authoritative supplement to Gratian, the Gregorian *Decretales* of 1234. Thus a new general legal culture was being born in the twelfth century—a veritable *ius commune*, a common law for the European Church—and with it a new profession open to the trained clerks who went on from their arts courses to degrees in law. Then, as now, the legal profession was seen by outsiders as a honey-pot, while for insiders it was a strict discipline with good prospects. By the time the *Carmina Burana* were compiled, every bishop had his curia and officials and every archdeacon his court. The learned law affected, some would say infected, every aspect of ecclesiastical life, and the older disciplines of confession and penance became judicialized. For some critics, the judicialization of the priestly office was a devaluation of the spiritual and the growth of ecclesiastical bureaucracy a scandal. Many poems in the *Carmina Burana* mirror this unease:

Postquam sedent iam securi,	Once established in their places,
contradicunt sancto iuri. [...]	they contradict the holy law. [...]
Domus dei fit spelunca.	God's house becomes a den of thieves:
Sunt latrones, non latores	Brigands they are, not bearers
legis Dei destructores.	of God's law, these destroyers of it.

(Ecce sonat in aperto, CB 10, 19-20, 22-23)

Or, as Walter of Châtillon put it,

'Date, vobis dabitur:	'Give and it shall be given unto you
talis est auctoritas' [...].	thus says the text' [...].
Hec est causa curie,	At the Curia it's the case
quam daturus perficit;	that he who pays wins:
defectu pecunie	for the want of money
causa Codri deficit.	Codrus[20] loses his action.

(Manus ferens munera, CB 1, 5, 1-2; 6, 1-4*)*

Walter was born in Lille, but is usually known as Walter of Châtillon because he taught at Châtillon for a short while before securing a comfortable position as *notarius* and *orator* to the powerful William of the White Hands, archbishop of Rheims, to whom he dedicated his epic poem *Alexandreis* (on Alexander the Great), finished *c.* 1175.[21] The extract just quoted comes from his *Manus ferens munera* ('Hands bearing gifts'), the very first poem in the *Carmina Burana*; but he developed the theme further in *Propter Sion non tacebo* ('I shall not be silent for Sion's sake', *CB* 41), where Sion is the personification of the Church. Probably composed 1171-73, it is another powerful invective against the corrupting power of money. The poem deplores the state of the Church in general and of the Roman Church in particular, which it likens to the ship-devouring waters of the straits of Messina (*vorax guttur Siculi*), where the monstrous *Scylla* (personification of advocates) and *Charybdis* (personification of the Chancery) lie in wait for innocent ships (representing appellants). The cardinals are pirates or treacherous sirens, led by *Bursa* (purse), and Franco (identified by Walther Holtzmann as the papal chamberlain)[22] is a grasping scrooge who is never satisfied. Yet in his fierce denunciation of grasping clerk and cardinal, Walter singles out two named persons for special praise:

---

[20] Juvenal's poverty-stricken poet (iii, 203).

[21] *PL*, CCIX (1855), 459-572.

[22] Walther Holtzman, 'Propter Sion non tacebo: Zur Erklärung von Carmina Burana 41', *Deutsches Archiv*, X (1953-54), 170-75.

Petrus enim Papiensis,	Peter of Pavia
qui electus est Meldensis	just elected to Meaux

(Propter Sion non tacebo, CB 41, 27, 1-2)

and

Alexander ille meus	my Alexander

(Propter Sion non tacebo, CB 41, 28, 4)

The first was a French clerk, Master Peter Ithier, educated at Orléans and Bologna, who enjoyed the kind of meteoric career only dreamed of (and parodied) by the anonymous authors of the *Carmina Burana*. The stages in his career—archdeacon (of Pavia and Chartres), (titular-) abbot (of St-André in Chartres), bishop (-elect of Meaux), and cardinal (cardinal priest of S. Crisogono), all in the space of ten years—read like the cherry-stone rhyme. Yet Walter describes him as a safe haven amidst the manifold dangers of the papal Curia:

Petrus enim Papiensis,	Peter of Pavia
qui electus est Meldensis,	just elected to Meaux
portus recte dicitur.	is justly called safe-haven.
nam cum mare fluctus tollit,	For when the sea raises up a storm
ipse solus mare mollit.	he alone can moderate the waves.

(Propter Sion non tacebo, CB 41, 27, 1-5)

The second was Pope Alexander III (1159-81), 'my Alexander', a patron and protector of educated clergy *(litteratos)*, who would be a true worshipper of God if he were not betrayed by the successors of Giezi, the prophet Elisha's mercenary and unscrupulous servant who accepted rich presents from Naaman the Syrian, when Elisha cured him of leprosy:

Ille fovet litteratos,	Educated men he favours,
cunctos malis incurvatos,	All bowed low by hardship
si posset, erigeret.	He would raise up, if he were able.
Verus esset cultor Dei,	God's true worshipper would he be,
nisi latus Elisei	If Giezi were not corrupting
Giezi corrumperet.	Elisha's servants.

(Propter Sion non tacebo, CB 41, 29)

At a more humorous level, the *Gospel according to the Mark of Silver* also satirizes the venality of the Roman court. It begins:

> At that time, the pope said unto the Romans, 'When the Son of Man comes before the seat of our majesty, first say to him, "Friend, wherefore art thou come?" And if he persists in knocking, without giving you anything, cast him into the outer darkness.'

and ends:

> First [the rich clerk] gave to the doorman, then to the chamberlain, then to the cardinals. When he saw the cardinals and ministers accepting many gifts from the clerk, the lord pope became sick unto death. Then the rich clerk sent him a potion of silver and gold, and he recovered immediately. Then the lord pope called the cardinals and ministers and said unto them, 'Brethren, let not any of you be deceived by empty words. I give you an example: as I take, go and take thou likewise.' *(CB 44)*

This play on St Matthew's gospel, as well as the audacious *Gambler's Mass*, complete with neumes (*CB* 215), appear shocking to modern eyes; but such parody reflects the capacity of medieval culture to combine the sacred and profane to an unusual degree. It is a literary echo of the juxtaposing of gargoyle and sacred image in a Gothic church or the interplay of seriousness and jocularity, some of it bawdy, found in the borders of manuscript books or in the misericords of monastic and cathedral choirs. One can sense the juvenile delight of young students in the daring parody of the religious forms which bounded their lives, as they laughed at the pretensions of their lords and masters and even made fun of the sacred texts of the gospels and the Mass. But they were not in fact revolutionaries. They wanted to join the escalator of office and benefice, gain a reliable patron, land a good appointment—all the while passing through the experience of adolescent emotion.

If the ecclesiastical world of the twelfth century was being transformed by the expansion of a money economy, so was the secular world. A rising population led to urban expansion; booming trade created new wealth, based not on land but on production and commerce, which required new financial institutions: international banking facilities, international credit and exchange. In the political world, too, the gifts and proffers gradually gave way to standardized payments; legal and administrative services became more widely available and offered for fees rather than as a favour. The issue of royal documents became a matter of routine, paid for by the recipient. In England, for example, the normal fee for an ordinary judicial writ was half a mark of silver (6/8d), at a time when an income of £20-£30 pounds (400-600 shillings) a year would keep a knight. Similarly, the papal chancery issued standard letters and privileges as a matter of course, but the petitioner had to pay for the labour and materials involved; and if a case had to be presented or a point argued, then proctors had to be employed and the patronage of powerful supporters invoked. If the intervention of the pope or of one of the cardinals was required, then proffers for access would be needed.

> First [the rich clerk] gave to the doorman, then to the chamberlain,
> then to the cardinals. *(CB 44)*

The schools themselves underwent a similar transition from free service to fee-based commerce, as rapid expansion opened the *studia* to ever-increasing numbers and a competitive market-place emerged, in which masters and students hired their lodgings, their lecture-rooms, and one another. So fierce was the scramble for space in Paris that in 1245 the University had to issue decrees against 'gazumping' and other unfair practices:

> No one shall outbid another by a higher price for classrooms which
> the other has rented. [...] No-one shall hire a house over the head
> of others, so long as those living in the house wish to occupy it.[23]

This commercialization, which paralleled the judicalization and bureaucratization of many aspects of contemporary society, raised fundamental moral questions. The practices of social intercourse

---

[23] Thorndike, *University Records*, p. 53.

emphasized gift-giving and gift-receiving, but where could the line be drawn between the ancient and expected courtesy of giving a present to a patron and the purchase of office or judgment? At what point did the customary proffer become a corrupting gift? Peter the Chanter, who taught generations of clerical students at Paris (including the future Pope Innocent III) in the last twenty years of the twelfth century, preached a rigorous attitude to such practices, holding up Thomas Becket of Canterbury and Lucasz of Esztergom in Hungary as twin models of incorruptibility in the discharge of their ecclesiastical offices.[24] But as the gifts and proffers of the past were being transformed into fees and taxes, their capacity to corrupt was reduced while their apparent commercialism was increased. Here the world and the Spirit came into direct confrontation. Theologians like Peter the Chanter held that the gifts of knowledge, grace, and justice should be freely bestowed on rich and poor alike; speaking of spiritual office, Walter of Châtillon wrote in *Licet eger cum egrotis* (*CB* 8, 4, 1-2),

Donum Dei non donatur,	The Gift of God cannot be given
nisi gratis conferatur.	except free of charge.

But the schools, the Church, and the courts required expensive infrastructures of scribes, clerks, record-keepers, proctors, and advocates. The emergence of fee-based bureaucracies, in which the beneficiary paid the costs, and tax-based governments, in which the population as a whole bore the expenses of administration, and fee-based schools, in which the students paid for their lectures and examinations, seemed to threaten the integrity of the Church, the government, the schools, and the law. The *Carmina Burana* graphically reflect the current unease over such developments. *Nummus* (money) and *munera* (gifts) make their appearance very early on in the satirical section. Money and gifts lubricate the wheels of justice, ease the path of the rich, grease the palms of patrons and judges:

---

[24] Baldwin, *Masters, Princes, and Merchants*, I, 181; II, 121 n. 46. Cf. John T. Noonan, *Bribes* (New York: Macmillan,1984), 'The Quarter and the Road', pp. 173-205.

Manus ferens munera	Hands bearing gifts
pium facit impium.	make the sacred blasphemous.

(CB 1,1, 1-2)

In terra summus rex est hoc tempore Nummus.
Today is Money high king over all the earth.
(In terra summus, CB 11, 1)

Money, as the sin of Simon Magus, buys its way into sacred office:

Simon sedens inter eos	Simon seated in their midst
dat magnates esse reos.	allows the great to litigate.
Simon prefert malos bonis [...].	Simon prefers bad men to good [...].
Simon aufert, Simon donat,	Simon takes and Simon gives,
hunc expellit, hunc coronat.	expelling this one, crowning that.

(Ecce sonat in aperto, CB 10, 25-27, 33-34)

The distinction between proffer and bribe, fee and purchase was not yet clearly drawn—and was always capable of confusion; and as the papal court came to depend on such payments, Walter of Châtillon's bleak picture of ravening beasts lying in wait to fleece unwary petitioners reflected contemporary disquiet. Just as every member of staff in a grand hotel—from the doorman to the chambermaid and the waiter—expects a tip, so did the door-keepers, the attendants, the recorders, and the scribes and advocates attached to royal, noble, episcopal, and papal courts. How far any of this constituted bribery or corruption is very much open to question; but its almost universal existence provided a ready target for critics and moralists.

The *Carmina Burana* reflect the ambiguities of this rapidly changing world and echo the concerns of contemporary critics like John of Salisbury, Stephen of Tournai, and Peter the Chanter of Paris. At the same time, they reveal the complex interplay of regional and linguistic influences, where the effects of courtly love, the Provençal lyric, and the goliardic cocking-a-snook at authority and custom mingled with parody, satire, tavern-songs, and even hymns to the Virgin. There is an uninhibited *joie de vivre* about the collection: *gaudeamus igitur, iuvenes dum sumus*—or, as *CB* 75 says:

Omittamus studia,	Down with study! Books away!
dulce est desipere,	Come and learn a sweeter truth
et carpamus dulcia	finding pleasure in the play
iuventutis tenere!	and the greenery of youth:
res est apta senectuti	it's the pride of old professors
seriis intendere	to engage in serious things
[res est apta iuventuti]	and the joy of youth (God bless us)
[leta mente ludere.]	to prefer venereous things.* 25

(Omittamus studia, CB 75, 1, 1-[8]).

While, never far away, there was the age-old knowledge that fate was fickle, life short, and there would be a final reckoning:

Lex carnalis et mortalis valde transitoria
Fugit, transit velut umbra, que non est corporea.
Quod videmus vel tenemus in presenti patria,
Dimittemus et perdemus quasi quercus folia.
Fugiamus, contemnamus huius vite dulcia,
Ne perdamus in futuro pretiosa munera!
Conteramus, confringamus carnis desideria,
Ut cum iustis et electis in celesti gloria
Gratulari mereamur per eterna secula! Amen.
(Iste mundus furebundus, CB 24, 5-13).

All our wheelings, all our dealings, truly transitory, must
Crack and crumble, totter, tumble, into insubstantial dust.
All we strive for, stay alive for, in our earthly entity
Will be shattered, lost and scattered, like old leaves blown from the tree.
Let us therefore, cease to care for worldly joys, and turn them down—
Lest in sorrow, we tomorrow, be denied our heavenly crown:
Let us bend to put an end to corporal cupidity—
That among the blessed number saved for immortality
We may merit and inherit life through all eternity. Amen.*

---

25 Cf. Walsh's translation in *Love Lyrics from the Carmina Burana*, p. 53: 'Let us forsake our studies; it is sweet to play the fool. Let us enjoy the delights of innocent youth. Devotion to serious things is appropriate for old age, but sport with a glad heart is the right course for youth.'

SELECTED BIBLIOGRAPHY

Facsimile

Carmina Burana. Facsimile Reproduction of the Manuscript Clm 4660 and Clm 4660a, edited by Bernhard Bischoff, Publications of Mediaeval Musical Manuscripts, 9 (Brooklyn, N.Y.: Institute of Mediaeval Music, 1967). Also available in a German version: *Carmina Burana. Faksimile-Ausgabe der Handschrift Clm 4660 und 4660a,* edited by Bernhard Bischoff (Munich: Prestel, 1967).

Editions and Translations

Carmina Burana, I: *Text.* 1: *Die moralisch-satirischen Dichtungen,* edited by Alfons Hilka and Otto Schumann (Heidelberg: Carl Winter, 1930); 2: *Die Liebeslieder,* edited by Alfons Hilka † and Otto Schumann (Heidelberg: Carl Winter, 1941; 2nd edition 1971); 3: *Die Trink- und Spielerlieder; Die geistlichen Dramen; Nachträge,* edited by Otto Schumann † and Bernhard Bischoff (Heidelberg: Carl Winter, 1970). II: *Kommentar.* Commentary by Alfons Hilka and Otto Schumann. 1: *Einleitung (Die Handschrift der Carmina Burana); Die moralisch-satirischen Dichtungen* (Heidelberg: Carl Winter, 1930; 2nd edition 1961). (Abbreviated as *CB.*)

Die Gedichte des Codex Buranus lateinisch und deutsch, translated by Carl Fischer and Hugo Kuhn (Zurich: Artemis, 1974; rpt Munich: Deutscher Taschenbuch Verlag, 1979).

Selections from the Carmina Burana: a verse translation, translated by David Parlett (Harmondsworth: Penguin, 1986; rpt 1988).

Thirty Poems from the Carmina Burana, edited by P.G. Walsh (Reading: University of Reading, Department of Classics, 1976; 3rd rpt 1983).

Carmina Burana, translated and edited by Clare Russell and Philip Pickett (London: the editors, 1978). – An edition of the texts for which medieval musical notation survives.

Further reading

Peter Dronke, *Medieval Latin and the Rise of the European Love Lyric,* 2nd edition, 2 vols (Oxford: Clarendon Press, 1968).

Stephen C. Ferruolo, *The Origins of the University: the schools of Paris and their critics, 1100-1215* (Stanford: Stanford University Press, 1985).

Stephen C. Ferruolo,' "Quid dant artes nisi luctum": Learning, Ambition and Careers in the Medieval University', *History of Education Quarterly*, XXVIII (1988), 1-22.

A.L. Gabriel, 'The Cathedral Schools of Notre-Dame and the Beginning of the University of Paris', in A.L. Gabriel, *Garlandia: studies in the history of the mediaeval university* (Notre Dame: The Medieval Institute, University of Notre Dame; Frankfurt: Knecht, 1969), pp. 39-64.

J.K. Hyde, 'Universities and Cities in Medieval Italy', in *The University and the City*, edited by Thomas Bender (Oxford: Oxford University Press, 1988), pp. 13-21.

P. Kibre, *The Nations in the Medieval Universities* (Cambridge, Mass.: Medieval Academy of America, 1948).

P. Kibre, *Scholarly Privileges in the Middle Ages* (Cambridge, Mass.: Medieval Academy of America, 1962).

Léo Moulin, *La Vie des étudiants au Moyen Age* (Paris: Michel, 1991).

G. Paré, A. Brunet and P. Tremblay, *La Renaissance du xiie siècle: les écoles et l'enseignement* (Paris: Vrin, 1933).

Olive Sayce, *The Medieval German Lyric 1150-1300* (Oxford: Clarendon Press, 1982).

R.W. Southern, 'The Schools of Paris and the School of Chartres', in *Renaissance and Renewal in the Twelfth Century*, edited by Robert Benson and Giles Constable (Cambridge, Mass.: Harvard University Press, 1982; rpt Oxford: Clarendon Press, 1985), pp. 113-37.

Jacques Verger, *Les Universités au moyen âge* (Paris: Presses universitaires de France, 1973).

Helen Waddell, *The Wandering Scholars*, 7th edition (London: Constable, 1934; rpt 1938; 1954).

Helene Wieruszowski, *The Medieval University: masters, students, learning* (Princeton: Van Nostrand, 1966).

LATIN SONGS IN THE *CARMINA BURANA:* PROFANE LOVE AND SATIRE

Peter Dronke

The period 1100-1230 is a high point in European lyrical poetry and music, both sacred and profane, in Latin and in several vernaculars. For Latin, we have many testimonies of religious lyric from the very beginnings of Christian worship in the West in almost every century, but Latin secular songs were not often written down in earlier times. Secular songs in the European vernaculars must also have existed at all periods, yet they were scarcely written down at all before the twelfth century. There was no vernacular reading public, with the small exception of Anglo-Saxon England. The aristocracy, in so far as they learnt to read and write, learnt it in Latin.

Certainly we must reckon with much secular lyrical composition in the earlier centuries which is simply irrecoverable. Yet also, so much more has survived from the twelfth century onwards because secular and profane impulses among poets became so much more marked. It was an age of new openness to a wider world, an age of humanism, a 'Renaissance'. The expression 'the Renaissance of the twelfth century' is so often used, and it must certainly be qualified, yet there is an undeniable element of truth there.

For profane lyrical compositions of the twelfth and early thirteenth centuries, the *Codex Buranus* is our most spectacular witness. It has 238 pages, and was compiled in the first third of the thirteenth century, perhaps chiefly in the decade 1220-30, with occasional later additions. The older view had been that it was from as late as 1300, but I tried, in one of my earliest essays, in 1962, to show that the attempts to see influences of late *Minnesang* in the collection were imaginary; at the same time, the great medieval art historian, Otto Pächt, confirmed my intuitions about the poetry by writing to me as follows:

The style of the miniatures allows us to date the *Carmina Burana* manuscript safely within narrow limits. One of the best authorities on German illumination, Albert Boeckler (*Deutsche Buchmalerei vorgotischer Zeit*, Königstein, 1952, pl. 61) dates it first third of the thirteenth century, and no art historian with any training could possibly disagree with this opinion. It suffices to point to the type of the female figures which is paralleled by the famous statues of Ecclesia and Synagoge of Strasbourg, i.e. works of 1220-1230. A late thirteenth-century date is out of the question.[1]

The significance of this is that the manuscript is uniquely close in time to the period of composition of many of the finest lyrics themselves. The great vernacular manuscript collections, by contrast, were mostly compiled many generations after the compositions.

The existence of bilingual texts in this manuscript, Latin/German and occasionally Latin/French, and again the many German strophes interspersed among the Latin ones, brings out graphically the interdependence of Latin and vernacular poets and composers, copyists and performers. The Latin lyrics are neither mere imitations, trailing behind the vernacular, as some scholars believed, nor are they always the source of inspiration, preceding the vernacular, as others have maintained. There was a fruitful give and take: exchanges between courtly and clerical and popular songs were an everyday occurrence and this codex is, in many ways, a record of such exchanges.

Where was it compiled? It was discovered in a monastery in Bavaria, Benedictobura, and so the collection became known as *Carmina Burana*, but it was not Bavarian, as the earlier scholars thought. In recent decades, the suggestions have been made of Southern Austria, somewhere above Trieste,[2] or again, nearer the Hungarian border, not far from Graz;[3] but

---

[1]   'A Critical Note on Schumann's Dating of the *Codex Buranus*', *Beiträge zur Geschichte der deutschen Sprache und Literatur*, LXXXIV (Tübingen, 1962), 173-83, at p. 181.
[2]   Bernhard Bischoff, *Carmina Burana: Einführung zur Faksimile-Ausgabe der Benediktbeurer Liederhandschrift* (Munich: Prestel, 1967), p. 16 (suggesting Carinthia).
[3]   Bernhard Bischoff, *Carmina Burana* I, 3: *Die Trink- und Spielerlieder; Die geistlichen Dramen; Nachträge*, edited by Otto Schumann † and Bernhard Bischoff (Heidelberg: Carl Winter, 1970), pp. xi-xii (suggesting Seckau).

the most convincing proposal has been the most recent one, made in 1983, of Northern Italy, above Trento, quite possibly at a foundation of canons in Bressanone, or Brixen.[4]

Several things speak in favour of this. There are some typically Italian spellings (in the Latin texts, for instance, the use of *z* instead of *c*, common in a lot of North Italian manuscripts), and also the North Italian style of the neumes—the indications of the musical line—not, unfortunately, on staves, but indications that served to remind singers of the melodies.

If this North Italian Tyrolese origin is right, then the range and provenance of the songs collected in the *Carmina Burana* is amazing.

A large number stem from Germany and Austria, but also a considerable range are French, especially from the cathedral school of Notre Dame in Paris, which, in the second half of the twelfth century, was a quite outstanding centre of polyphonic as well as of monodic music. Two at least of the songs stem from Spain (one of which is discussed in some detail below). One of the most famous songs in the codex, the Archpoet's 'Confession', this drinking song which is also an apologia for the Bohemian artist's way of life, was composed in North Italy, in Pavia, in 1163. This coexistence in a single manuscript of songs from all over the Continent is a dramatic illustration of the internationality of medieval lyric.

For whom was this manuscript copied? It is, with its eight miniatures, relatively a de luxe manuscript. It is not a *codex aureus*, a codex full of gold leaf, such as was presented at times to a king or emperor or pope,

---

[4] Georg Steer, '*Carmina Burana* in Südtirol. Zur Herkunft des Clm 4660', *Zeitschrift für deutsches Altertum*, CXII (1983), 1-37. Most recently, Olive Sayce, *Plurilingualism in the Carmina Burana: a study of the linguistic and literary influences on the Codex*, Göppinger Arbeiten zur Germanistik, 556 (Göppingen: Kümmerle, 1992), has argued on linguistic grounds that, of the two principal scribes in the codex, the first 'is an Italian speaker, with some rudimentary knowledge of Old French and German, living in an area where German was spoken and German texts copied', and that 'the second scribe can be shown to be a Romance speaker, but in this case all the evidence, direct and indirect, indicates that his native tongue is the *langue d'oïl* of Northern France. There are, however, also distinct traces of an Italian influence' (pp. 62-63).

yet it is a precious, rather than everyday, manuscript. If we imagine the canons at Bressanone as the scribes, was it produced for their own pleasure or, as I think more probable, did they have a great patron—a humanistic, highly educated nobleman or a bishop with worldly tastes? The patron must have travelled widely, or have had many links with courts and cathedral schools throughout Europe, for so disparate a repertoire to be assembled.

The collection shows elements of careful ordering. The pages were misbound in more modern times and there are some anomalies in the original ordering as well. But basically, there were in that original design, first, some fifty or so of the songs that scholars call 'moral-satirical'—the songs which respond to topical and political situations, which can attack the problems and vices of the age, and attack venality: even the Pope and the Roman Curia are not spared. Many of these survive as well, with full music, particularly in Notre Dame manuscripts from Paris.

Then there are some one hundred and twenty love-songs, for Latin lyric by far the largest collection of these. A number of subsections can be seen here. There is a group which have to do with Troy—with Dido and Aeneas, for instance. There is a group of dance-songs, which are signalled by their refrains and, sometimes, by their allusions to dancing. Then there is a large group that are followed by a German stanza in the same form and melody as the Latin, technically a *contrafactum*. Often it is uncertain which is the earlier, whether the form and melody come from the vernacular or the Latin. These hybrid pieces were for performance in a milieu where not all the listeners or performers will have been familiar with the learned language. We must imagine a situation in which students, who had been schooled in Latin, and young women, who had not, would be singing and dancing and flirting in the context of performing these songs.

Then we have, thirdly, some thirty-five songs which are 'goliardic', in the sense that has been made popular since Helen Waddell's *The Wandering Scholars*: the irreverent parodies of hymns and prayers and liturgies, songs that celebrate drinking, gambling, and a riotous, anti-establishment way of life.

Finally, there are seven religious plays on New Testament themes. That last section, the only one which contains specifically religious material, makes one wonder whether, in parts of the manuscript which today are lost, there might have been a whole section of religious lyric; but there is no evidence for this, though it cannot be ruled out.

In addition, we have, among the lyrical verses, some in non-lyrical metres, like classical hexameters (not for singing but for reading or reciting), sometimes proverbial wisdom, sometimes mythography, sometimes satire. This is a very unusual feature in this manuscript. Quite often, again, there are some neumes over the lyrics, from which a melody can be reconstructed, or identified if it survives elsewhere in fully legible form.

Now, from among nearly two hundred secular Latin lyrics, I must choose. I cannot hope to evoke the full imaginative and artistic range, but I hope that the five songs that I have chosen (three complete, two in extract only) will constitute an invitation to the *Carmina Burana,* and suggest why these songs are still so captivating today.

My first example is a love-song that reveals its secrets only gradually. It is copied twice in the *Codex Buranus* (the second time with elaborate neumes), and also in the early thirteenth century in a manuscript from Barcelona, where it has fully legible music and, interestingly, a different conclusion.[5]

---

[5] For the citation of lyrics below, I have relied on the facsimile edition of the *Codex Buranus: Carmina Burana. Faksimile-Ausgabe der Handschrift Clm 4660 und 4660a,* edited by Bernhard Bischoff (Munich: Prestel, 1967), though taking account also of *Carmina Burana* I, 2: *Die Liebeslieder,* edited by Alfons Hilka †and Otto Schumann (Heidelberg: Carl Winter, 1941)— to which I refer readers for the extensive critical apparatus—and of *Carmina Burana: Texte und Übersetzungen,* edited by Benedikt Konrad Vollmann, Bibliothek des Mittelalters, 13 (Frankfurt am Main: Deutscher Klassiker Verlag, 1987). The first piece (*CB* 85 in these two editions) occurs in the *Codex Buranus* (= B) fol. 36*v* and again on fol. 64*r*. The Spanish MS, which I use for the fourth strophe, is Escorial Z.II.2, fol. 287*r*. (This reads 'viterem' and 'exxilio', but, *pace* Hilka/Schumann, 'pro scribis' is written as two words rather than one). At 3, 2, both copies in B, but also the Spanish codex, read 'virgines'.

Veris dulcis in tempore
florenti stat sub arbore
Iuliana cum sorore.
    Dulcis amor!
    Qui te caret hoc tempore
    fit vilior.

In the time of gentle spring,
underneath a flowering tree,
Juliana and her sister stand.
    Gentle love!
    Whoever lacks you at this time
    loses nobility.

Ecce florescunt arbores,
lascive canunt volucres,
inde tepescunt virgines.
    Dulcis amor!
    Qui te caret hoc tempore
    fit vilior.

Look how the trees begin to flower,
seductively the birds are singing—
with this the girls grow less cold.
    Gentle love!
    Whoever lacks you at this time
    loses nobility.

Ecce florescunt lilia,
et virginum dant agmina
summo deorum carmina.
    Dulcis amor!
    Qui te caret hoc tempore
    fit vilior.

Look how the lilies burst into flower,
and hosts of young girls offer up
songs to the highest of the gods.
    Gentle love!
    Whoever lacks you at this time
    loses nobility.

'Si viderem quod cupio,
pro scribis sub Exilio,
vel pro regis filio!
    Dulcis amor!
    Qui te caret hoc tempore
    fit vilior.'

'If only I could see the one I long for,
whom I'd exchange for all the scribes in Silos,
or even for the king's son!
    Gentle love!
    Whoever lacks you at this time
    loses nobility.'

[In the *Codex Buranus*, the last strophe reads:

Si tenerem quam cupio
in nemore sub folio,
oscularer cum gaudio.

If only I could hold her whom I long for,
in the grove, under the leaves,
I would kiss her joyfully.]

The Spring opening for a love-song is very common, but very uncommon is the naming of the beloved, of the girl in love. The refrain—signalled 'Refl.' at the words 'Qui te caret [...]'— brings us to one of the leitmotifs of courtly love poetry: that love has an ennobling power, that whoever lacks love lacks nobility. 'The highest of the gods' is not the Christian God but Amor. 'Carmina' may even have the suggestion, beyond 'songs', of 'spells'— magic invocations of the god. I think the final strophe in the Spanish manuscript is an example of one of the songs these girls sing. Silos, at Burgos, was one of the great Spanish abbeys of the high Middle Ages. In the *Codex Buranus* there is a different ending and it is clearly a man who sings.

Which is the original ending? I think there can be little doubt. The whole of the first three strophes describes the awakening emotions of the two girls, Juliana and her sister. There is no mention of a man's love in these. The abrupt introduction of a strophe in which a man sings of love in the *Carmina Burana* version came about, I think, because the local allusion from Spain to the scribes of Silos was not understood in the Austrian or North Italian world when the song was written down, having made its way there.

Juliana, or her sister, cannot see the man she longs for—only the scribes in Silos, or possibly the king's son. Silos, at Burgos in Castile, was very close in the later twelfth century to a royal convent of Cistercian nuns called Las Huelgas, which served not only for the aristocratic nuns but also for well-born girls, who would go there for a time as a kind of finishing-school, before returning to secular life.

We have, from a later period, *c.* 1325, a great musical manuscript, the *Las Huelgas Codex*, which includes not only lyrics from Notre Dame, such as we have in the *Carmina Burana*, but also local songs, both profane and sacred, satirical and religious, which were composed most probably by the women of Las Huelgas themselves. So this song, though it survives isolated in a much earlier codex, was quite possibly composed by a woman poet in the convent of Las Huelgas, perhaps using the reference to the scribes in Silos in order to tease Juliana and her sister, who are not heroines from a romance but will probably have been members of the community there.

One other feature of this song, I believe, indicates its Spanish provenance. In Mozarabic Spain, for several centuries, women had sung, in Arabic or Hebrew, songs known as *muwashshahs*, in a form which is quite similar to that of this Latin song. Strophes with triple structure and rhyme go on to a verse which leads into the refrain and then the refrain itself, which rhymes with that earlier verse. I know that in Northern Europe there are similar forms (the *virelai* in France, the *carole* in England), but the *muwashshah* had one very unusual feature: it had a final strophe, known as the *kharja*, and this strophe was one in which the girl who performed the song sang in her own person and sang something which was amorous, witty, piquant, irreverent in some way, provocative. I would suggest that the final strophe here is, we might say, Juliana's *kharja*. It is a witty Latin counterpart to the closing strophes of the Mozarabic songs.

From this world of amorous springtime make-believe and urbane wit, let us turn to a more complex lyric, the savage song of a jealous lover who has lost his beloved. The melody does not survive.

Rumor letalis	The deadly gossip
me crebro vulnerat	wounds me over and over:
meisque malis	it piles new sorrows
dolores aggerat;	on my calamities;
me male multat	it hurts me badly,
vox tui criminis,	the talk of your lewd fault,
que iam resultat	now echoing
in mundi terminis.	to the ends of the earth.
Invida Fama	Envious Rumour
tibi novercatur:	is a stepmother to you:
caucius ama,	be more cautious in your loving,
ne comperiatur!	lest it be divulged!
Quod agis, age tenebris,	Whatever you do, do in darkness,
procul a Fame palpebris!	far from the lids of Rumour's eyes!
Letatur amor latebris	Love delights in hidden places,
cum dulcibus illecebris	with its soft lures
et murmure iocoso.	and playful murmuring.
Nulla notavit	You weren't marked
te turpis fabula	by any base slander
dum nos ligavit	while we were bound
amoris copula,	by the bond of love;
sed frigescente	yet as soon as our
nostro cupidine,	desire had grown cold,
sordes repente	at once you demean yourself
funebri crimine!	in deadly vice!

Fama, letata	Rumour, thrilled

Fama, letata
  novis hymeneis,
irrevocata
  ruit in platheis.
Patet lupanar omnium
pudoris in palatium,
nam virginale lilium
marcet a tactu vilium
  commercio probroso.

Nunc plango florem
  etatis tenere,
nitidiorem
  Veneris sydere,
tunc columbinam
  mentis dulcedinem,
nunc serpentinam
  amaritudinem.
Verbo rogantes
  removes hostili,
munera dantes
  foves in cubili.
Illos abire precipis
a quibus nichil accipis—
cecos claudosque recipis,
viros illustres decipis
  cum melle venenoso.[6]

Rumour, thrilled
  by your new matings,
beyond recall
  rushes through open streets.
A brothel for all encroaches
on the palace of innocence,
for the virginal lily
is withered by the touch of vile men
  in their traffic of shame.

Now I weep for the flower
  tender in years,
more radiant
  than Venus's star,
weep for her mind's
  dovelike sweetness then,
weep for her serpentine
  bitterness now.
Men who ask for love
  you drive off with a harsh word,
men who bring you gifts
  you warm in your bed.
You order them to go away
if you get nothing from them—
you welcome the blind and the lame
and delude illustrious men
  with your poisoned honey.

This astonishing fantasy of love and hate conjoined is unlike anything else in the love-lyrics of the age. I would see it as a dramatic creation, depicting the progression of the disappointed lover into delusion, hysteria, and paranoia. The first stanza moves from self-pity and wild hyperbole ('your shame has gone to the ends of the earth') to ironic advice ('Be more cautious—do it in the dark!').

---

[6] *CB* 120: B fol. 50*v*; I have also collated a photo of Stuttgart HB I 95, fols 77*v*-78*r*.

In the second strophe, the poet shows up through his persona the hypocrisy, the double standard in love for women and men ('It was fine as long as it was with me. With others, you're just a prostitute.'). The man can choose freely, the woman, if she chooses, at once becomes sordid, 'sordes repente'.

The final strophe begins nostalgically, sentimentally we might say, but ends in paranoia. The poet uses two biblical allusions in a parody that is not humorous, but ferocious. Christ (Matthew 10.16) told his apostles they should be doves in their innocence but also serpents in their cunning. Here, the woman is seen as the dove who has become the serpent. The traditional paradox, as old as Sappho, that love is bitter-sweet (γλυκύπικρον), both poison and honey, is here turned against her—she who welcomes the blind and the lame for money yet drives away 'illustrious men' (and by this the enraged lover clearly means himself). But do the blind and the lame really have money to spend on prostitutes? I think here too we see the hint of madness in the hyperboles, and here again the allusion is a grim biblical parody. It was Christ who welcomed the blind and the lame, but the poet depicts his faithless mistress as a parody of Christ, as Buñuel in his film depicts Viridiana, welcoming into her house the cripples and beggars, whose orgy is portrayed as a wild echo of the Last Supper.

My third example is from Song 165 in the *Carmina Burana*, the opening verses of a love-lyric that begins as a prayer to the god Amor or Cupid:

Amor, telum
  es insignis Veneris,
voluntates
  mentis gyrans celeris,
  amantum afflictio,
cordis fibras
  elicis et conteris!
Vultu sereno
  clarior pre ceteris,
  me tibi subicio [...][7]

Amor, you are the weapon
  of wondrous Venus,
you who swiftly whirl about
  the intentions of the mind,
  torment of lovers,
you pluck out and then destroy
  the fibres of the heart!
You, serene of countenance,
  more radiant than the other gods,
  I subject myself to you [...]

---

[7] B fol. 66*v* (with 'est' for 'es' in the second verse cited).

The love-songs in the *Carmina Burana* are filled with the gods of pagan classical mythology, and especially Amor and Venus feature again and again. The songs as a whole seem to avoid allusions to the Christian God. As a great scholar from the beginning of the century, Wilhelm Meyer, said: 'the medieval poets created a freer path for themselves by setting their love-songs in the realm of ancient mythology.'

But was this a purely rhetorical freedom, a playful use of something learnt in the schools? Or was there an element of belief as well? Certainly, medieval intellectuals regarded the planetary gods, Jupiter, Venus, Mars, Mercury and the rest, as Intelligences moving the spheres, and therefore as angels or messengers of the supreme Christian God, bringing down his influences on the sublunary world. Again, in the twelfth and thirteenth centuries, we have many magic spells and incantations which are copied, especially ones to Venus, and they are not set down out of antiquarian or folkloristic interest: they are clearly copied for practical purposes, to be used for persuading a reluctant girl to yield.

I think that in the *Carmina Burana* songs the degrees of play and of belief, in Venus or Amor or other pagan gods, can vary, and yet that there can also be an underlying serious insight. The prayer to Amor here, for instance, conveys the paradox of the lover's desire. While the arrows of his love, his *tela Veneris*, are aimed at his beloved, they afflict him within himself just as painfully. He is both an Amor Cupido, a personified love and desire, and the victim of Amor Cupido. In desire, there is an element of responsibility, but also of helplessness—just as in Euripides, in the *Hippolytus*, for instance, Aphrodite is both the force of passion within Phaedra herself and a force greater than herself that makes Phaedra suffer remorselessly and dooms her.

With my fourth example, poem *CB* 131, we turn from *Amor* to *Caritas*, the Christian love of neighbour, and from love-songs to one of the most passionate of the satires in the *Carmina Burana*. This is not humorous satire, it is harsh, even elegiac. We know who the poet was: Philip the Chancellor, Chancellor of Notre Dame in Paris, embattled defender of the University of Paris against the friars, who wanted to take it over, and against the Archbishop of Paris. Philip went even as far as Rome to try and persuade the Pope of the justice of his cause, though Rome gave him no satisfaction. There, as he puts it, the Pope thunders fulminations, denunciations. His priests leave the wounded man to bleed to death. In the house of Romulus, that is in the papal Curia in Rome, charity is not to be found:[8]

Dic, Christi veritas,	Tell me, you truth of Christ,
dic, cara raritas,	tell me, loved rareness,
dic, rara caritas,	tell me, rare love,
ubi nunc habitas?	where do you live now?
Aut in valle visionis,	In the valley of vision,
aut in trono Pharaonis,	or on Pharaoh's throne,
aut in alto cum Nerone,	or on high with Nero,
aut in antro cum Timone?	or with Timon in his cave?
Vel in viscella scyrpea	Or is it in the bulrush basket,
cum Moyse plorante?	with Moses crying?
Vel in domo Romulea	Or in the house of Romulus,
cum Bulla fulminante?	with the Pope's Bull fulminating?
Respondit caritas:	Love answered:
'Homo, quid dubitas?	'Man, why do you have doubts?
Quid me sollicitas?	Why do you harass me?
Non sum quod usitas,	I am not what you meet every day,
nec in euro nec in austro,	neither in the East nor South,
nec in foro nec in claustro,	not in marketplace or cloister,
nec in bysso nec in cuculla,	not in fine linen or in cowl,
nec in bello nec in bulla:	not in war or papal Bull:
de Iericho sum veniens,	I am coming from Jericho,
ploro cum sauciato,	weeping with a wounded man,
quem duplex Levi transiens	whom a pair of priests, passing by,
non astitit grabato.'[9]	did not help to find a bed.'

---

[8] B fol. 54*r-v* (interspersing strophes of *CB* 131a). The song also survives in eight other MSS, and in three sixteenth-century printed anthologies of Flacius Illyricus. It is only Flacius who preserved (or restored) the correct reading in st. 1: 'aut in antro cum Timone', and not 'cum Theone', as is printed by the modern editors. Both Schumann/Bischoff and Vollmann identify this 'Theon' as a holy hermit called Theonas—but that Philip should have accused such a holy man, along with Nero, of lack of charity is hardly credible. Philip will have known about Timon of Athens especially from Cicero's *De amicitia* (23, 87), but his copyists, less learned than he, must soon have garbled the verse.

In the first strophe, the impassioned rhetorical questions rise to a crescendo. All the places, all the people show where charity is not. The 'valley of vision' is Isaiah's terrifying image of slaughter and treading underfoot; Pharaoh and Nero are the high and mighty arch-oppressors; yet the misanthropic Timon of Athens, skulking in his cave, has no more charity than they. If the exposed baby Moses, crying, roused pity in Pharaoh's daughter, the fulminating Pope is pitiless. All this is stressed again by the personified Charity in her answer, and yet that answer, at the close, also implies a gleam of hope: even if the priests, devoid of charity, pass the wounded man by, the audience knows that there was a Samaritan, one of that race whom the priests despised, who behaved differently.

My final example, *Stetit Puella*, is a brief, enigmatic song that includes some words of German amid the Latin. We have looked at songs celebrating *amor*, erotic love, and just now at a song celebrating *caritas*, love of neighbour. *Stetit Puella* brings *amor* and *caritas* together. No medieval melody survives, but the first two strophes have been set by Carl Orff.

Stetit puella	A girl stood
rufa tunica—	in a red dress—
si quis eam tetigit,	if anyone touched it,
tunica crepuit—eia!	the dress crackled—eia!
Stetit puella	A girl stood
tamquam rosula:	like a little rose,
facie splenduit	radiant of face
et os eius floruit—eia!	and her lips flowering—eia!

---

[9]   The third strophe ('O vox prophetica [...]') is not cited here: it is filled with rather complex topical allusions, about which I offer some notes in the booklet to Sequentia's recording *Philippe le Chancelier* (RD77035, Harmonia Mundi, 1990), in which the song can be heard complete.

Stetit puella	A girl stood
bi einem boume,	beside a tree,
scripsit amorem	she wrote her love
an einem loube:	upon a leaf:
dar chom Venus also fram.	then at once Venus came.
Caritatem magnam,	Great charity,
hohe minne	high courteous love
bot si ir manne.[10]	is what she gave her man.

Here 'eam' in the first strophe can mean 'if anyone touched *it*' or 'if anyone touched *her*'. Likewise 'manne' in the third may mean her lover, but it could just as easily mean her husband.

The sound 'eia' can be tender, as in a lullaby, or melancholy, like a lover's 'heigh-ho', or exultant, like 'hurrah', in drinking songs. It can be used to represent the hee-haw, the donkey's bray in the processional of the ass in the medieval feast of fools; or again, it can express awestruck admiration, as I think it does here. Today the equivalent of this 'eia' might be 'Wow!'

The first strophe suggests to me that the girl in the red dress, which crackles if it, or she, is touched, is sensually alluring and that, even without meaning to, she arouses the desire of men who see her and, seeing, long to touch. Yet the second strophe shows that she is not trying to be provocative: she is in love with someone, and that love flowers in her radiance.

Filled with ardour, she writes her love, or her lover's name, on a leaf, and the writing brings Venus, erotic love, forth: we might say, it liberates the feelings that had blossomed within. And those feelings are, inseparably, *caritas* and *hohe minne*, charity and the height of courtly love, which, thanks to the grace of Venus, the girl in the red dress can bestow upon 'her man'—quite possibly her husband.

The song as we have it stems from a highly educated poet and a refined world. Yet it alludes to and draws upon two quite different

---

[10] *CB* 177: B fol. 70*r*. In the twelfth verse, B has 'an eimē lovbe'.

traditions. Scholars have seen the first strophe as an early example of a widespread German riddle, and indeed even as a small child in Germany I was still taught to sing a version of such a riddle:

Ein Männlein steht im Walde	A little man stands in the forest
ganz still und stumm;	all still and mute;
es hat von lauter Purpur	he wears a little cloak
ein Mäntlein um [...]	of purple red [...]

In the next verses comes the question:'Who can he be, this little man who stands all alone on one leg in the forest with his little purple red cloak?' The answer, in the riddle I was taught, was that it is a reddish mushroom, the one that the French call *petit rouge* or the Germans *Rotkäppchen*; some scholars have suggested that in the Latin text it was an onion: if the red dress is something that crackles to the touch, it could well be an onion skin. Yet the second strophe in the Latin song shows that this allusion, even if it is present, cannot be the poet's principal intention—that it is a girl, and not a mushroom or an onion, that he has in mind. We cannot interpret the whole song, as some scholars have tried to do, as an example of the riddle.

Similarly, the third strophe has been interpreted as the girl's performing of a piece of love magic, writing on a leaf so as to conjure up Venus and win a man. There are good parallels in magical texts, especially from Late Antiquity, and again, the poet may well be aware of such connotations. Yet he insists that *this* girl does not need such magic. She has got 'her man'—she has already won him, and Venus is the force, within her as much as outside her, that enables her to show him that love uninhibitedly.

It is the nature of the love evoked that is the most remarkable aspect of this song. A friend of mine in Yale, Ingeborg Glier, Professor of Medieval German there, once began a lecture on courtly love, which I do not think she has ever published, by pointing out that this song breaks all the rules that modern scholars have laid down about medieval love.

The cliché goes that medieval men and women were taught that *amor* and Venus were evil, and were the very opposite of *caritas*; and medievalists assure us that high courtly love was incompatible with married love, and just as incompatible with Christian charity. If this poet had sat an exam on courtly love poetry today, he would undoubtedly have failed! Yet all the loves that the scholars enjoin us to keep separate, this poet wanted to bring together. He refused to see them as incompatibles. It is because of this that his little song is profound as well as delightful; it also means that in a few words this lyric can evoke for us something of the whole gamut of what desire and love could mean in the world of the *Carmina Burana*.

THE GERMAN TEXTS IN THE *CODEX BURANUS*

Cyril Edwards

All manuscripts are unique, but some are more unique than others: the *Codex Buranus* is a manuscript that invites superlatives. The reader who approaches it from a knowledge of Carl Orff, or from a more specialized point of view, from an acquaintance with recordings of medieval music or with the many anthologies containing its lyrics, finds himself surprised by the variety of German material that the codex contains. It is a *Sammelhandschrift*, a collective or compendium manuscript, but even among manuscripts of this character it is uniquely heterogeneous. It is an anthology, or, to be more accurate, several anthologies in one. Not only is it the most comprehensive and important anthology of medieval Latin verse, but it is also the earliest anthology of German lyrics. Peter Dronke has shown that it is the second largest collection of medieval Latin plays;[1] it is moreover an important marker in the growth of medieval German drama. Even this does not exhaust the German material; the codex provides, in effect, a fascinating cross-section of the uses of the written vernacular, sacred and profane, in the thirteenth century.

That century saw a consolidation of processes we can identify as part of the twelfth-century renaissance in France and Germany; the vernacular continued to gain ground and to be put to a widening range of uses. The German texts in the codex are in a number of different hands which range in date from *c.* 1230 to the early fourteenth century. The extent of the use of the vernacular varies tremendously: sometimes only one word in an otherwise Latin text is in German; on the other hand, there are texts of some length entirely in the vernacular. This is not untypical of the bilingual nature of learning in the thirteenth century.

---

[1] Peter Dronke, *Nine Medieval Latin Plays* (Cambridge: Cambridge University Press, 1994), p. 195.

However, as the recent work of Olive Sayce and Ulrich Müller has emphasized, the *Codex Buranus* is uniquely polylingual, involving, apart from medieval Latin and Middle High German, Old French, Old Provençal, Greek, and Italian.[2] This mix of languages is, as we shall see, partly functional, partly ludic—for aesthetic effect.

At its most functional, the interrelationship between Latin and German can be seen in the form of interlinear glosses. On fol. 56*r* two Latin poems list names of birds, *Nomina auium* (*CB* 133), and of beasts, *De nominibus Ferarum* (*CB* 134). The names are accorded their vernacular equivalents in the form of glosses, translations written above the line, in the same way as the modern-day student of foreign languages annotates his paperbacks [pl. 18]. Clearly the vernacular here serves an educational purpose, teaching the reader the meaning of the Latin nouns. A glance at the standard editions of the *Carmina Burana* is misleading here, for they miss the bilingual point, either omitting the German glosses or relegating them to footnotes. German interlinear glosses date back to the Carolingian period, when they were used, for example, to teach monks the Benedictine Rule.

The two glossed lists are related to the preceding poem, *CB* 132 *Iam vernali tempore*, which consists for the most part of lists of birds and beasts and their respective sounds. The origins of these poems are contentious. Part of *CB* 132 is to be found in the sixth-century *Anthologia Latina*. August Reifferscheid was of the view that all three poems may have originated in a lost encyclopaedia of natural history known as the *Pratum* or *Prata* of Suetonius (*c*. AD 69-*c*. 140).[3] The

---

[2] Ulrich Müller, 'Mehrsprachigkeit und Sprachmischung als poetische Tendenz: Barbarolexis in den *Carmina Burana*', in *Europäische Mehrsprachigkeit. Festschrift zum 70. Geburtstag von Mario Wandruszka*, edited by Wolfgang Pöckl (Tübingen: Niemeyer, 1981), pp. 87-104; Olive Sayce, *Plurilingualism in the Carmina Burana: a study of the linguistic and literary influences on the Codex*, Göppinger Arbeiten zur Germanistik, 556 (Göppingen: Kümmerle, 1992).

[3] Suetonius Tranquillus, Gaius, *Praeter Caesarum libros reliquiae*, edited by August Reifferscheid (Leipzig: Teubner, 1860; rpt 1971), pp. 258-59; 308-12. Reifferscheid's view of the lyrics as 'versified Suetonius' is contentious.

Pratum is a highly problematic work. Known to us only by allusions in Late Antique authors such as Isidore and Priscian, its content can only be reconstructed on the basis of medieval fragments of anonymous authorship. Werner Wegstein is of the view that *CB* 133 and 134 are twelfth-century in origin, both where the glosses and the Latin poems are concerned. He adduces palaeographic and linguistic evidence in support of this theory: none of the manuscripts can be dated with any certainty prior to the twelfth century, and some of the medieval Latin words would seem to be back-formations from medieval German. At the latest count, over eighty-four manuscripts contain these lists, a high proportion of them with glosses.[4]

German here is clearly subordinate to Latin. At the opposite end of the linguistic spectrum stand a number of texts entirely in German, which were written towards the end of the manuscript and on the leaves now known as the *Fragmenta Burana* (Clm 4660a), leaves which fell out when the manuscript was rebound; these later additions were rediscovered and edited by Wilhelm Meyer in 1901. They show a greater degree of autonomy, vernacular culture working more independently of Latin.

On fol. 110*v* (*CB* 17*), interpolated between the pages of the longer of the two passion plays in the codex, there is a whole page of aphorisms, entered in a hand of the late thirteenth or early fourteenth century. These 'Sprüche' are from the collection attributed to Freidank. The Freidank transmission begins in the late twelfth century and is enormously complex, involving over fifty manuscripts, both Latin and vernacular branches, and continuing in printed form into the sixteenth century. Sebastian Brant in 1508 concluded his printed version with the words: 'Man hielt etwan vff kein spruch nicht / Den nit herr frydanck

---

[4]   Werner Wegstein, 'Zur Überlieferung der "Versus de volucribus, bestiis, arboribus" ', in *Studia Linguistica et Philologica. Festschrift für Klaus Matzel zum sechzigsten Geburtstag*, edited by Hans-Werner Eroms et al. (Heidelberg: Carl Winter, 1984), pp. 285-94. I am indebted to Richard Wilson (Birkenhead) for discussion of the problems relating to these texts; the lines of transmission between the medieval poems and their hypothetical classical sources are far from clear.

het gedicht' ('No saying then was worth a jot / unless by Master Freidank wrote').[5] For the most part the work now known as Freidank's *Bescheidenheit* consists of loosely related aphorisms. Some passages more narrative in character are concerned with corruption in Rome, others describe the diplomatic crusade of 1228-29 to Acre, in which not a blow was struck, but Frederick II had himself crowned king of Jerusalem, only to be pelted with dung and entrails by the local populace. The fifty-six lines of Freidank in the *Codex Buranus* are of a more general character. Most of them relate to the habits of animals, insects, and birds, but in contrast to the glossed Latin poems they resemble condensed beast fables: 'Gienge ein hunt des tages tausent stunt / ze chirchen, er ist doch ein hunt' ('A dog may go to church a thousand times a day, / but a dog he'll stay').[6] Others describe the miseries of being in love: 'Swer lieb hat, der wirt selten urei / vor sorgen, daz ez unstæte sei' ('If a person's in love he's seldom free / of worry about inconstancy'). We know next to nothing of Freidank; the *Annales Caesariensis* record that a certain 'Fridancus magister' died in 1233 [pl. 19].

On fol. 1r of the *Fragmenta Burana*, an unpractised Bavarian hand of the late thirteenth or early fourteenth century, h[14], has entered *CB* 7*, a translation of the first fourteen verses of St. John's Gospel [pl. 20]:

In anegenge was ein wort, daz wort was mit got, got was daz wort.
vnd was in anegenge mit got. von im sint alliv dinch gemachet an
in ist gemachet nicht. swaz mit im ist gemachet daz ist daz ewige
leben. daz ewige leben ist ein liecht den livten, daz liecht daz

---

[5] See Berndt Jäger, *Untersuchungen zur Überlieferung und Rezeption Freidanks im Spätmittelalter*, Göppinger Arbeiten zur Germanistik, 238 (Göppingen: Kümmerle, 1978).
[6] Quotations from the codex are based upon *Carmina Burana: Texte und Übersetzungen*, edited by Benedikt Konrad Vollmann, Bibliothek des Mittelalters, 13 (Frankfurt am Main: Deutscher Klassiker Verlag, 1987), with emendations based upon the facsimile edition, *Carmina Burana. Facsimile Reproduction of the Manuscript Clm 4660 and Clm 4660a,* edited by Bernhard Bischoff, Publications of Mediaeval Musical Manuscripts, 9 (Brooklyn, N.Y.: Institute of Mediaeval Music, 1967).

liuchtet in der vinster, div vinster mach sein nicht begreiffen. Ein
mennisch wart gesant von gote des name was Johannes. der chom
zv̊ einer geziuchnv̊sse daz er geziuch were des liechtes er was
nicht daz liecht niwer daz er gezivch were des liechtes. daz ware
liecht ist daz daz ein igesleichen mennisch erlivchtet der in disiv
welt bechumt. er cham in div welt div welt erchant sein nicht. er
cham in sein aigen lant die seinen enpfiengen sein nicht aver die
in da enpfiengen den gab er den gewalt daz si gotes chint wi̊rden,
vnd die an seinen namen gelavpten die warn nicht geworn von
wollv̊ste des plůtes noch von wollv̊ste des vlaisches wan svnder
von gote. daz wort ist ze vlaische worden vnd wont in vñs wi̊r
haben sein ere gesehen als eines ainworn sunes wie den sein vater
eret voller genaden vnd voller warheit—durch disiv rede des hailgen
ewangelii vergebe vñs vñser herre alle vñser missetat. Amen

(In the beginning was a word, the word was with God, God was
the word. And was in the beginning with God. By him are all things
made, without him nothing is made. Whatever is made with him is
eternal life, eternal life is a light to the people, the light that shines
in the dark, the dark cannot encompass it. A man was sent by God
whose name was John. He came to give witness, that he might be
a witness of the light. He was not the light; he was only a witness
of the light. The true light is that which enlightens every person
who comes into this world. He came into the world, the world did
not recognize him. He came into his own land; his people did not
accept him. But to those who did accept him he gave the power to
become God's children, and those who believed in his name were
not born of the lust of the blood nor of the lust of the flesh but
separately of God. The word has become flesh and lives in us. We
have seen his glory as that of a single-born son, how his father
honours him full of grace and full of truth.—By the virtue of these
words of the holy gospel forgive us, our Lord, all our sins. Amen.)

This translation shows no dependence on the surviving translations
from the Carolingian period, the two Old High German versions of the
Diatessaron, the Fulda Tatian translation and Otfrid von Weissenburg's
rhymed gospel harmony. Translations of parts of the Bible into German
prose are exceedingly rare in the thirteenth century. The words that are

appended to this translation are the words spoken after the reading of the gospel in the mass. The text may have been intended for use in church, a bridge between clerical learning and the laity. However, the evidence for such liturgical practice in the Middle Ages is limited; it does not seem to have been the norm before the fifteenth century.[7]

Other possibilities have been suggested: because of the importance it attaches to the power of the word, *logos*, John 1.1-14 came to be used frequently as a charm or amulet, a usage which persisted into modern times. Its magical powers were thought to guarantee a good harvest or to ward off the perils of childbirth; this belief persisted into modern times. A third, intriguing possibility was mooted by Anton Schönbach: John 1.1-14 was frequently translated into the vernacular because it was a text of vital importance to the heretical sect known as the Cathars.[8] It formed part of their most important rite, the *consolamentum*, and was recited when a new member was admitted to the sect in Carcassone. The crux for the Cathars was John 1.3: 'Omnia per ipsum facta sunt: et sine ipso factum est nihil, quod factum est.' The Cathars interpreted this verse dualistically, to suggest that by 'nihil' ('nothing') was meant this world, which was created not by God, but by the principle of evil. The perfectus Petrus Auterii, active in the Toulouse area in the first decade of the fourteenth century, maintained that the words mean: 'All that is created exists without God.'[9] This

---

[7] *Deutsche Philologie im Aufriß*, edited by W. Stammler, 2nd edition (Berlin: Schmidt, 1960), II, 883-86; Adolph Franz, *Die kirchlichen Benediktionen im Mittelalter* (Freiburg im Breisgau: Herdersche Verlagshandlung, 1909), II, 57.

[8] Anton E. Schönbach, 'Studien zur Geschichte der altdeutschen Predigt. Drittes Stück: Das Wirken Bertholds von Regensburg gegen die Ketzer', *Sitzungsberichte der kaiserlichen Akademie der Wissenschaften zu Wien, philosophisch-historische Klasse*, vol. CXLVII (1904), 93-97.

[9] Hans Christoph Stoodt, *Katharismus im Untergrund: Die Reorganisation durch Petrus Auterii 1300-1310*, Spätmittelalter und Reformation, Neue Reihe, 5 (Tübingen: Mohr, 1996), pp. 78-79. See also Alexander Patschovsky, 'The literacy of Waldensianism from Valdes to *c.* 1400', in *Heresy and Literacy, 1000-1500*, edited by Peter Biller and Anne Hudson, Cambridge Studies in Medieval Literature, 23 (Cambridge: Cambridge University Press, 1994), pp. 112-36 (esp. pp. 132-36); and in the same volume, Peter Biller, 'The Cathars of Languedoc and written materials', pp. 61-82, esp. p. 68. I am indebted to Nigel Palmer for drawing my attention to this volume.

belief is attacked in a sermon of Berthold von Regensburg (1210-72), the greatest German preacher of the thirteenth century. Schönbach argues that the *Codex Buranus* translation is Cathar in origin; the conclusive point for him is the omission in the translation of John 1.10 of 'et mundus per ipsum factus est' ('and the world was created by him'). This may have been an accidental omission—the hand is unpractised and does make errors. Schönbach's attempt to link this text with the Cathars of Provence is less than convincing, as the translation is quite clearly in a later hand and in a Bavarian dialect which is markedly different from that of the first scribe, who appears familiar with the Provençal lyric.[10] If this text is of heretical origin, then it is more likely to stem from the quill of a Waldensian. The sect of the Waldensians was active in the late thirteenth century in south-east Germany. The importance they attached to *In principio*, a text which German Cathars named the *anegenge* after the second word, is attested by Berthold von Regensburg, who in 1263 was entrusted with the task of preaching against heresy and embarked on a preaching tour of Germany, France, and Switzerland in 1263-64. Berthold died in 1272. The text was probably written down a little later. Its isolated nature in the *Fragmenta*, backed by an unrelated Latin love poem (*CB* 8*), makes it impossible to contextualize it. The Waldensians were forced by the Inquisition to go underground; the hypothesis that the text may be of Waldensian origin is therefore as irrefutable as it is attractive.

Less problematic are the German texts which form part of the dramatic material in the codex; these clearly serve as a bridge between Latin and the vernacular, opening the plays to a wider audience. On the last leaf of the codex proper, 112v we find *CB* 23* *Cantus Ioseph ab Arimathia*, in a late-thirteenth- or early-fourteenth-century hand, h[35]. The *cantus*, neumed throughout, is a duet in German between Joseph of Arimathea and Pilate, in which the former asks permission to bury Christ and the latter agrees. Each is accorded an eight-line strophe. The duet would fit well into either of the two passion plays in the codex and was probably added to the manuscript for that reason.

---

[10] Sayce, *Plurilingualism*, p. 14.

It would perhaps best fit the *Ludus breviter de passione* (*CB* 13*), which ends on fol. 4*v* of the *Fragmenta*, with a sequence of stage directions, including: 'Tunc veniat ioseph ab arimathia et petat corpus iesu. Et permittat pilatus.' ('Then let Joseph of Arimathea come and request the body of Jesus. And let Pilate permit it.')

Another text in the *Fragmenta* is *CB* 15* (fols. 5*r*-6*v*), the Benediktbeuern Easter Play, *Ludus immo exemplum Dominice resurrectionis*. The soldiers guarding the tomb against the possibility of the corpse being taken by the disciples are accorded a song of six stanzas. The first stanza is sung by the chorus of the five soldiers, entirely in Latin. Then they sing solos, five stanzas of four rhymed lines. The last line of each stanza is a mixture of German and Latin: 'schăwe propter insidias.' ('Beware of treachery.') The middle man, 'Tercius miles', in addition sings his first half-line in German: 'SHaw̆e alumbe ne fures veniant.' ('Look out everywhere, lest thieves come.') The extra German words are placed in the middle stanza, symmetrically. Their effect is dramatic, presumably comic. But why German here, and only here? It is the only scene in the play in which the soldiers appear as individuals; elsewhere, in chorus, in Latin, they ask for money for guarding the tomb and tell Pilate of the resurrection. Conceivably, type-casting is at work here. The soldiers have bit parts; they may well have been known to the audience. If it was thought appropriate to put German into their mouths, this may have been because they were of the laity. (In the closely related Klosterneuburg Easter Play, the performance ends with the singing of the German hymn *Christ, der ist erstanden*.)

The largest proportion of vernacular in the plays is in the longer of the two passion plays, *CB* 16*, towards the end of the main part of the manuscript. Those familiar with Carl Orff will recognize the lyric *Chramer gip die varwe mier*, which Orff smuggles into the German texts he sets to music in the section of the *Carmina Burana* entitled *Uf dem anger*, 'in the meadow'. This is not, as the Orff-lover might expect, an erotic song, but is, initially, a celebration of the delights of this world by Mary Magdalene. In the scene portraying the encounter of Mary with the grocer, the *mercator*, the Magdalene is portrayed as a

Lady World figure. *Fro Welt* was a popular subject in the sculpture and literature of the early thirteenth century. Her fair front and foul behind grace the portal of the cathedral of Worms and form the subject of a song by Walther von der Vogelweide (*fl. c.* 1190-*c.* 1230), *Fro welt, ir sult dem wirte sagen* (L. 100,24). The text of the Magdalene's song is neumed, and it has been possible to reconstruct a melody from a 'parallel manuscript', a Vienna Passion Play of the fourteenth century (Cod. Vind. 12887 (Suppl. 561)). This is the only authentic medieval tune that Orff employs in his German section.

Mary Magdalene celebrates the delights of the world, *mundi delectatio*, initially in Latin, and then addresses the grocer, again initially in Latin. This scene with the grocer, the 'Krämerszene', was to become a pivotal scene in German medieval drama, developing from the most slender biblical basis (John 12.3: 'Then took Mary a pound of ointment of spikenard, very costly'; Mark 14.3: 'a woman having an alabaster box of ointment of spikenard very precious'). The Benediktbeuern grocer boasts to Mary of his wares, again in Latin, but she then bursts into German song:

MARIA MAGDALENA: Chramer, gip die varwe mier,
div min wengel roete,
da mit ich di iungen man
an ir danch der minnenliebe noete!

ITEM: Seht mich an, iungen man,
lat mich ev gefallen!

ITEM: Minnet, tugentliche man
minnekliche vråwen!
minne tuôt ev hoech gemût
vnde lat evch in hoehen eren schåuven.
REFL. Seht mich an, iunge man [. . .]

ITEM: Wol dir werlt, daz du bist
also vreudenreiche!
Ich wil dir sin vndertan
durch dein liebe immer sicherlichen. [. . .]

TUNC ACCEDAT AMATOR, QUEM MARIA SALUTET, ET CUM
PARUM LOCUNTUR, CANTET MARIA AD PUELLAS:

> Wel dan, minneklichev chint,
> schǎwe wier chrame!
> chauf wier die varwe da,
> di vns machen schoene vnde wolgetane.
> er muez sein sorgen vře,
> der da minnet mier den leip.

ITERUM CANTET: Chramer gip die varwe mier [...]

MERCATOR RESPONDET:

> Ich gib ev varwe, deu ist guǒt,
> dar zuoe lobelich,
> dev eu machet reht schoene
> vnt dar zuoe uil reht wnnechliche.
> nempt si hin, hab ir si,
> ir ist niht geleiche.

(MARIA MAGDALENA: Grocer, give me make-up / to make my
cheeks blush, / so that I can compel the young men / to love me
against their will. REFRAIN: Look at me, young fellows, / May
you find me pleasing!

Men of worth, love / charming ladies! / Love will inspire high
spirits in you / and make you appear of high repute. REFRAIN:
Look at me, young fellows [. . .]

Hail to thee, world, / so rich in pleasure that thou art! I shall be thy
true subject, / bound to thee in love forever. [. . .]

THEN A LOVER IS TO APPROACH, WHOM MARY IS TO
GREET, AND AFTER THEY HAVE CONVERSED A LITTLE,
LET MARY SING TO THE GIRLS:

Come on then, charming maidens, / let us see the grocer's wares!
/ Let us buy make-up there / which will make us beautiful and
handsome. / He who is to love me / must be free of all care.

LET HER AGAIN SING: Grocer, give me make-up [...]

LET THE GROCER REPLY: I'll give you make-up, good stuff, /
of high repute; / it'll make you truly beautiful / and absolutely
charming to boot. / Take it, keep it, / there is nothing like it.)

The first line, 'Chramer, gip die varwe mier', is a direct translation of the Latin sung earlier: 'Michi confer venditor', but then the song goes its own way, invoking the doctrine of courtly love, which has an odd ring in the mouth of a fallen woman. Mary proclaims her allegiance to this world, again employing imagery familiar from the courtly love lyric: 'Ich wil dir sin vndertan'—what C.S. Lewis termed the 'feudalisation of love'.[11]

Mary Magdalene has three dreams, in each of which an angel appears to her announcing the presence of the Saviour. After the first dream she wakes up and cheerfully sings of the delights of this world again, in Latin. Her lover's arrival prompts Mary to make another visit to the grocer for more make-up; this time her song is in German, addressed to her girl-friends, with the *mercator* replying in German. Having procured her make-up, she falls asleep again, the dream is repeated, and again she wakes up full of the joys, singing *Mundi delectatio*. This is the last time she is to wake up so cheerfully. The singing apparently exhausts her, and she falls asleep again. The third dream brings about her *conversio*. She wakes up to curse her previous life, and the angel welcomes her to the fold. She casts off her secular adornments and dons black, whereupon her lover backs off, as does the Devil, who has presumably been lurking in the background throughout, although no stage-direction mentions him until this point.

Later in the play, the Magdalene addresses Christ in German quatrains and sings a bistrophic lament in German after Jesus has forgiven her sins. The Virgin Mary, at the Cross, sings a four-strophe lament in German, elaborately neumed. The last character to speak in German is Longinus, who sings a couplet as he pierces Christ's side: 'Ich wil im stechen ab daz herze sin / daz sich ende siner marter pin.' ('I shall pierce his heart / to put an end to his pangs of torture.') The merchant, both the Maries, and Longinus all sing or speak in both German and Latin. Christ and the angels know only Latin. The use of German is at times clearly for dramatic effect, but it is not employed consistently. The bilingual plays in the *Codex Buranus* mark a halfway stage in the evolution of medieval German drama, between the exclusively Latin plays of the twelfth century and the vernacular plays of the later Middle Ages. This linear view is, however,

---

[11] C.S.Lewis, *The Allegory of Love* (Oxford: Clarendon Press, 1936).

something of an over-simplification, as plays continued to be written and performed in Latin throughout the Middle Ages.

The bulk of the German material in the manuscript consists of texts written by hands of *c.* 1225-50. The texts for the most part are entered after a Latin text, and the relationship between Latin and German is problematic. Broadly speaking, the entering of the German strophes would appear to have been inspired by either a thematic or a metrical resemblance to the preceding Latin text, suggesting in some cases that the Latin and German lyrics were sung to the same melody. With one exception these texts are lyrics; the exception that further broadens the generic spectrum is *CB* 203a, on fol. 90*v*, strophe 69 of the *Eckenlied* [pl. 21]:

> Vns seit uon Lutringen Helfrich
> wie zwene rechen lobelich
> ze saemine bechomen:
> Erekke unde ovch her Dieterich;
> si waren beide uraislich,
> da uon si schaden namen.
> als uinster was der tan
> da si an ander funden.
> her Dietrich rait mit mannes chraft
> den walt also unchunden.
> Ereke der chom dar gegan;
> er lie da heime rosse uil; daz was niht wolgetan.

(Helfrich of Lutringen tells us / how two warriors of high repute / encountered one another: / Erec and Lord Dietrich; / they were both fearsome, / and suffered in consequence. / Dark was the fir wood where they found one another. / Courageously Dietrich rode / through the unfamiliar forest. / Erec came thither on foot; / he left many horses at home; that was an error on his part.)

The *Eckenlied* belongs to the loosely associated cycle of Dietrich epics, whose hero is Dietrich of Bern, a legendary figure inspired by the historical Theodoric the Great (AD 454-526), the Ostrogothic king who invaded Italy and ruled there from 493 to his death. He entered German folk memory in association with Attila the Hun and plays a background role in the only heroic lay to survive from Carolingian times, the *Hildebrandslied*. Dietrich plays a more dominant role in the tragic climax of the *Nibelungenlied*, written down for the first time *c.* 1200. The Dietrich epics form a successor to the heroic epic, an often burlesque portrayal of heroic deeds. The hero Ecke, who is mentioned in a number of epics in the cycle, has no historical counterpart; he may derive his name from that of the sword of Dietrich, Eckesahs.[12] The *Eckenlied* tells how the young giant—on foot, since no horse can carry him—challenges Dietrich in a forest in the Tyrol and is ultimately beheaded. The recent hypothesis tracing the origins of the *Codex Buranus* to the Tyrol, advanced by Georg Steer,[13] may be adduced to explain the inclusion of this strophe in the manuscript. Scribe and audience alike would have found the subject of interest, and the detailed topography of the epic suggests that it was indeed composed in the Tyrol.

The strophe in the *Codex Buranus* constitutes the earliest evidence for the *Eckenlied*; the transmission is divergent and diffuse. The opening suggests that Helfrich von Lutringen (Lorraine) was or was believed to be the author of the epic. In the story Helfrich figures as another victim of Dietrich who warns Ecke of impending disaster; he also appears elsewhere in the cycle.[14] Clearly there is some muddle here, and the suggestion that the *Carmina Burana* text formed an alternative opening to the *Eckenlied* is attractive. The opening formula is reminiscent of the first strophe of the *Nibelungenlied*: 'uns ist in alten mæren wunders vil geseit' ('in old tales many wonders are told to us'), emphasizing the oral tradition that may well antedate the written version.

The *Eckenlied* strophe occurs after the bulk of the German love-lyrics in the main hands. Dietrich epics do not otherwise occur in the same manuscripts as medieval German lyrics;[15] this would suggest that

---

[12] George T. Gillespie, *A Catalogue of Persons named in German Heroic Literature* (Oxford: Clarendon Press, 1973), p. 33

[13] Georg Steer, '*Carmina Burana* in Südtirol. Zur Herkunft des clm 4660', *Zeitschrift für deutsches Altertum*, CXII (1983), 1-37.

[14] Gillespie, *Catalogue*, p. 67.

the compiler turned at this point to a different manuscript. The preceding Latin song is a drinking song, *Hiemali tempore* (*CB* 203). Horst Brunner discovered in 1970 a melody for the *Eckenlied* in Meistersinger manuscripts of the late Middle Ages, and this melody, it has been suggested, also fits the Latin song, though which has priority is open to question.[16]

Despite the diversity of the German texts in the manuscript, it is perhaps surprising that at first sight there is no sign of interest on the part of the compilers in the new genre most in vogue in the first half of the thirteenth century, the Arthurian romance. Such interest existed, however, and it takes the unusual form of scribal error. The scribe h[2], unfamiliar with the relatively obscure hero Ecke, has corrected the name to that of a hero more familiar to him, the hero of the earliest German Arthurian romance to survive, *Erec*, adapted by Hartmann von Aue in the late twelfth century from the romance of Chrétien de Troyes. At first the scribe writes 'EreKKe', an odd spelling, then more confidently 'EreKe'. Olive Sayce seeks here a French connection, a knowledge of Chrétien's *Erec et Enide*,[17] but the orthography renders that unlikely. The confusion between heroes may have been reinforced by the important role played by horses in the Arthurian romance. The manuscript transmission of Hartmann's *Erec* is freakish; the entire text is preserved only in the sixteenth-century Ambraser Handschrift, whereas only fragments of earlier date survive. But the popularity of the romance

---

[15] See Joachim Heinzle, *Mittelhochdeutsche Dietrichepik: Untersuchungen zur Tradierungsweise, Überlieferungskritik und Gattungsgeschichte später Heldendichtung*, Münchener Texte und Untersuchungen zur deutschen Literatur des Mittelalters, 62 (Munich: Artemis, 1978).

[16] Horst Brunner, 'Epenmelodien', in *Formen mittelalterlicher Literatur. Festschrift S. Beyschlag zum 65. Geburtstag*, Göppinger Arbeiten zur Germanistik, 25 (Göppingen: Kümmerle, 1970), pp. 149-68; for this and other melodies see *Carmina Burana. Lateinisch-deutsch. Gesamtausgabe der mittelalterlichen Melodien mit den dazugehörigen Texten*, edited by Michael Korth, René Clemencic, and Ulrich Müller (Munich: Heimeran, 1979).

[17] Sayce, *Plurilingualism*, p. 78.

in early thirteenth-century Bavaria is confirmed by the references to the text in Wolfram von Eschenbach's *Parzival*. Further south, Thomasin von Zerklaere, an Italian writing in German in the 1220s, also shows knowledge of Erec and Enit. The earliest fragment of *Erec* to survive from the area is fragment V (Niederösterreichisches Landesarchiv, Nr. 821), dating from the last third of the fourteenth century.[18]

The German lyrics are the best-known, but also the most contentious texts in the manuscript. The *Codex Buranus* is the oldest manuscript to contain a substantial number of German lyrics, over fifty of them. Ten of the strophes are attributed to named poets in the major compilation manuscripts of the late thirteenth and first half of the fourteenth century; the *Codex Buranus* itself does not name authors, with the exception of Der Marner, author of the two Latin poems *CB* 6* and 9*. With one exception (*CB* 143a, Reinmar e 360), all the strophes by identifiable authors are contained in the biggest of the later anthologies, the Manesse Codex or Große Heidelberger Liederhandschrift (C), which was compiled *c.* 1300. The probability is that the compilers of the *Codex Buranus* had before them a similar collection to the Manesse manuscript; they appended single German strophes, or sometimes a pair of strophes, to the Latin texts that they copied. They are not mere fillers; the German texts are not relegated to the bottom of the page or the margins. In the course of the century or so after the writing of the main part of the manuscript they were amended and corrected by later hands, showing a continuity of interest.

Where the named poets are concerned, the compiler shows the taste of a connoisseur. Five of the great names of *Minnesang* are represented: Dietmar von Eist, Reinmar der Alte, Walther von der Vogelweide, Heinrich von Morungen, Neidhart von Reuental. Dietmar von Eist is held to belong to the first generation of named poets, associated with the Danube area; he may be identical with a Dietmar who died in 1171.

---

[18] Hartmann von Aue, *Erec*, edited by Alfred Leitzmann and Ludwig Wolff, 6th edition by Christoph Cormeau and Kurt Gärtner, Altdeutsche Textbibliothek, 39 (Tübingen: Niemeyer, 1985), pp. XI-XII.

CB 113a is the first strophe of one of Dietmar's *Wechsel*, a genre in which lovers address each other *in absentia*, the strophes divided symmetrically between them. The lady laments: 'Vvaz ist fůr daz senen gůt, daz wip nah liebem manne hat?' ('What can assuage the sorrow a woman feels on account of her dear beloved?')

The acknowledged master of 'classical' *Minnesang*, Reinmar der Alte, an Austrian poet who died before 1210, is represented by three strophes. *CB* 143a is the first strophe of a joyous proclamation of a lady's love: 'Ze nⁱwen vrŏden stat min můt / hohe sprah ein schŏne wip.' (' "My mind is exalted, inclined to new joys," / said a beautiful woman.') 147a is again a first strophe, in which the female voice addresses a messenger who has come from her beloved: 'Sage, daz ih dirs iemmer lone: / hast du den uil lieben man gesehen?' ('Tell me, and I shall always reward you for it: / have you seen that most dear man?') The lyric belongs to the genre of the *Botenlied*, the messenger song. *CB* 166a 'Solde auer ich mit sorgen iemmer leben, / swenne ander lůte weren fro?' ('Am I to live forever in misery, / whilst other people rejoice?') is the first strophe in manuscript C of a male lover's lament, the dominant genre of *Minnesang* and the genre in which Reinmar excelled—*semper dolens, semper Reinmar*. Curiously, in manuscript A, the Kleine Heidelberger Liederhandschrift, the oldest of the three major later anthologies, this song is attributed to Gedrut, a shadowy figure whose name suggests that she was the only female *Minnesänger*. All the strophes attributed to her are in the male voice. Such multiple attributions are not uncommon in *Minnesang*.

Reinmar's Austrian rival, the most versatile of the *Minnesänger*, Walther von der Vogelweide, is also represented by three strophes. Two of these (*CB* 151a and 169a) are from one of his love-lyrics, a song of courtly love set in Maytime: 'Muget ir schouwen / waz dem meien / wunders ist beschert?' ('Can you see / what wonders have been bestowed upon May?') Seven pages of the Benediktbeuern manuscript separate these strophes; neither is the first strophe. (In manuscript A the song is ascribed to Lutolt von Seven.) This illustrates well the random selection process that the Benediktbeuern compilers seem to have employed. The third Walther strophe (*CB* 211a) is the opening verse of what, to judge from the manuscript transmission, was his most popular lyric, a crusading song, the 'song of Palestine', in which Walther imagines himself setting foot in the Holy Land:

> Nu lebe ich mir alrest werde,
> sit min sůndeg vge sihet
> daz schône lant, unde ouch div erde,
> der man uil der eren gihet.
> nu ist geschehen des ih da bat:
> ich pin chomen an die stat,
> da got mennischlichen trat.

(Now my life for the first time seems to me worthy, / since my sinful eye beholds / the beautiful land, and the very soil / that is so venerated. / Now that for which I prayed has come to pass: / I have come to the place / where God walked in human form.)

Whether Walther did ever go on a pilgrimage or a crusade is a moot point. The strophe follows a Latin drinking song, *Alte clamat epicurus* (*CB* 211). None of the strophes is accorded musical notation, but the discovery of the Münster Walther fragments (Staatsarchiv ms. VII 51) yielded an authentic medieval tune for both the drinking song and the 'Palästinalied'. The melody is certain; less convincing is the theory that Walther's strophe is intended as a parody of the drinking song.[19]

Heinrich von Morungen, identifiable as a Thuringian knight who died in 1220, achieved an originality in his imagery unsurpassed by his contemporaries. He is represented in the codex by the opening, male-voice strophe of a *Wechsel*, an unusual expression of ecstasy on the part of the male in love (*CB* 150a):

> Ich pin cheiser ane chrone
> vnd ane lant: daz meine ih an dem můt;
> ern gestůnt mir nie so schone!
> wol ir libe div mir sanfte tůt!
> daz machet mir ein vrowe gůt.
> ich wil ir iemmer dienen mer—
> ih engesah nie wip so wol gemůt.

---

[19] *Carmina Burana. Lateinisch-deutsch*, edited by Korth et al., p. 198; Müller, 'Mehrsprachigkeit', p. 104.

(I am emperor without a crown / and without lands: I mean as regards my state of mind; / never was I in such a splendid mood! / Praised be her person who makes me so happy! / It is a worthy lady who does this. / I shall serve her forever— / never did I see a lady of such a beautiful disposition.)

The fifth great German poet in the manuscript is Neidhart von Reuental, a younger contemporary and rival of Walther von der Vogelweide in the Austro-Bavarian area. Neidhart's songs are for the most part bucolic depictions of the summer festivities and winter barn-dances of peasants who interrelate with the more aristocratic persona of Neidhart himself, extraordinarily vivid oddities quite unlike anything in 'classical' *Minnesang*. They were resented for their popularity by Walther von der Vogelweide, who evidently felt himself upstaged. The single strophe in the *Codex Buranus* (*CB* 168a) is the opening strophe of one of Neidhart's two crusading lyrics:

> Nu grvnet auer div heide,
> mit grvneme lobe stat der walt;
> der wider chalt
> twanch si sere beide;
> div zit hat sich verwandelot.
> ein senediv not
> mant mich an der guten
> von der ih ungerne scheide.

(Now the heath blossoms again, / the wood stands in green leaf; / cold winter / oppressed them both; / the season has changed. / Languishing sorrow / reminds me of the good lady / from whom I am loath to be parted.)

The strophe is a *Natureingang*, a 'nature introduction', celebrating the return of spring. With a sudden switch of theme characteristic of Neidhart, the second strophe, not in the *Carmina Burana*, turns to the problems of the Germans on crusade. The crusade in question may be the ill-fated expedition to Damietta (1217-19), or perhaps that of Frederick II, the diplomatic crusade of 1228-29 criticized by Freidank.

If the generally accepted dating of the main hands of the codex is correct, then Neidhart is the poet in fashion.

A sixth poet whom we can identify by name, Otto von Botenlauben, has been the subject of a massive recent study.[20] With the exception of 'Kaiser Heinrich', the Emperor Henry VI, to whom manuscripts B and C attribute three lyrics, Otto is the best documented of the *Minnesänger*. Born between *c.* 1175 and 1180 of the prominent Frankish family of the Henneburgs, he inherited the now largely ruined castle of Botenlaube. It is thought that he participated in Henry VI's crusade in 1197; his presence in Sicily is attested in 1197. After the death of Henry VI, Otto remained in the Holy Land, where at some point before 1206 he married Beatrice of Courtenay, daughter of Joscelin III, seneschal of Jerusalem. It would seem that Otto spent most of the years between 1197 and 1217 in the Holy Land. From 1208 onwards he was linked with the Knights of St John. In 1220 Otto and Beatrice sold their possessions in the Holy Land to the Order of Teutonic Knights, and Otto returned to Germany. They made extensions to their castle of Botenlaube, but from 1231 onwards their concerns took a new direction. They sold their rights to the castle and founded in 1231 the Cistercian nunnery of Frauenroth. It looks as if they decided to devote their last years to religious causes, though it is not clear whether either or both of them renounced the world altogether. The last record of Otto is in 1244; by the beginning of 1245 Beatrix was a widow.

The single strophe by Otto in the Benediktbeuern codex (*CB* 48a) is the only German strophe in the hand of h[1], the main hand of the codex. It is on fol. 14*r*, some forty pages from the next German strophe. (It is also preserved in the smaller Heidelberg anthology A, where it is attributed to a poet called Niune, another case of multiple attribution; in the Manesse Codex it is attributed to Botenlouben.) It is the second strophe of an *alba*, a dawn-song, in which the lady speaks to her lover, bewailing his imminent departure. As dawn breaks, he has to leave to escape the prying eyes of the court:

---

[20]   *Otto von Botenlauben: Minnesänger, Kreuzfahrer, Klostergründer*, Bad Kissinger Archiv-Schriften, 1, edited by Peter Weidisch (Würzburg: Schöningh, 1994).

Hôrstu friunt den wahter an der cinne,
wes sin sanch veriach?
wir můzen uns schaiden nu, lieber man.
also schiet din lip nu jungest hinnen,
do der tach ůf brach,
unde uns diu naht so fluhteclichen tran.
naht git senfte, we tůt tach.
owe hercelieb in mach
din nu uerbergen niht.
uns nimit diu freude gar daz grawe lieht—
stand ůf riter!

(Do you hear, lover, the watchman on the tower, / hear what his
song said? / We must part now, dear man. / You left here like this not
long ago, / when day broke / and night divided us so fleetingly. /
Night soothes, day hurts. / Alas, my heart's love, I cannot / conceal
you now. / The grey light is taking all our joy away— / Get up, knight!)

There are two examples of this comparatively rare genre in the codex,
the other being the anonymous *CB* 183a:

Ich sich den morgensterne brehen—
nu helt, la dich niht gerne sehen.
uil liebe, dest min rat:
swer tougenlichen minnet,   wie tugentlich daz stat,
da frivnschaft hůte hat.

(I see the morning star breaking forth— / now, knight, do not let
yourself be seen if you can avoid it. / My most dear one, this is my
advice: / when lovers love in secret, how worthy it is / if that love
is well guarded.)

Both these lyrics refer to the watchman, a figure perhaps stemming
from the Provençal *alba*. The anonymous lyric may be the first strophe
of a dawn-song, or it may be a monostrophic lyric, complete in itself,
with its own aphoristic moral.

The fourteen lyrics attributed in other manuscripts to Otto von
Botenlauben show considerable variety in genre and in metrical form.
In the latter respect they bridge two phases of *Minnesang*: on the one
hand, Otto composed monostrophic lyrics consisting of *Langzeilen*, the

Germanic long lines characteristic of the earliest period of German love-lyric; on the other, he cultivated the Romance-influenced polystrophic, tripartite form of the *canzona*. It may be that his lyrics were composed over a considerable length of time, perhaps even in two distinct phases. In the Holy Land Otto would have had no German audience to speak of; perhaps his *canzonas* were composed after his return.

The same mix of long lines and *canzonas* confronts us when we come to look at the *anonyma* in the *Codex Buranus*. These are, as Olive Sayce points out, 'of unequal value',[21] with the weaker lyrics generally being in the later, *canzona* form. It is tempting to conclude with Sayce that some at least of these are pallid imitations, perhaps by the compiler or scribe, but this is not susceptible of proof.

As with the lyrics attributable to named poets, there is a wide variety of genres, but the value of the anthology lies in the emphasis it places on genres which are sparsely represented in the later collective manuscripts. The overt eroticism of the dawn-song constitutes a break from the central genre of the lover's lament, with its emphasis on unfulfilled, distant, courtly love; the other genre that moves in a similar direction is the *pastourelle*, depicting an open-air erotic encounter. There are two German *pastourelle* strophes in the manuscript, *CB* 142a and 163a. The latter shares a nonsense refrain with its Latin predecessor:

> Eine wunechliche stat
> het er mir bescheiden,
> da die blůmen unde gras
> stůden grůne baide.
> dar chom ich als er mih pat—
> da geschach mir leide.
> lodircundeielodircundeie!

(A delightful spot / he'd picked out for me, / where the flowers and grass / both grew green. / There I came as he requested me—/ sorrow befell me there. / Lodircundeie! Lodircundeie!)

---

[21]   Olive Sayce, *The Medieval German Lyric 1150-1300* (Oxford: Clarendon Press, 1982), p. 234.

The German *pastourelles*, like the anonymous *alba*, seem complete in themselves, monostrophic miniatures.[22]

Another rare genre among the *anonyma* is the woman's voice lyric, the *Frauenstrophe* or *Frauenlied*, a genre cultivated at an early stage in the Middle Ages in many European vernaculars.[23] *CB* 145a is a monostrophic example [pl. 22]:

> Uvere diu werlt alle min
> von dem mere ŭnze an den rin,
> des wolt ih mih darben,
> daz chunich von engellant
> lege an mine[n] arme[n].

(If the whole world were mine / from the sea to the Rhine, / I would gladly renounce it, / if only the king of England / lay in my arms.)

Two correctors, m[2] and k[5], have modernized the final idiom, changing the singular 'an minem arme' into the plural; more significantly, a later, fourteenth-century scribe, k[1], has emended the lyric, changing 'chunich' ('king') to 'diu chŭnegin' ('queen'), so that the poem shifts genre, becoming the more fashionable male lover's lament rather than a woman's voice lyric.[24] There has been much speculation as to the identity of the king or queen of England; one possibility is that the king might be Richard the Lionheart.

---

[22] For a broader discussion of the German and macaronic *pastourelles* see Cyril W. Edwards, 'Die Erotisierung des Handwerks', in *Liebe in der deutschen Literatur des Mittelalters. St. Andrews-Colloquium 1985*, edited by Jeffrey Ashcroft, Dietrich Huschenbett, and William H. Jackson (Tübingen: Niemeyer, 1987), pp. 126-48, and Cyril Edwards, 'Von Archilochos zu Walther von der Vogelweide. Zu den Anfängen der Pastourelle in Deutschland', in *Lied im deutschen Mittelalter: Überlieferung, Typen, Gebrauch. Chiemsee-Colloquium 1991*, edited by Cyril Edwards, Ernst Hellgardt, and Norbert H. Ott (Tübingen: Niemeyer, 1996), pp. 1-25.

[23] See *Vox feminae: studies in medieval woman's songs*, edited by John F. Plummer, Studies in medieval culture, 15 (Kalamazoo, Mich.: Medieval Institute Publications, Western Michigan University, 1981)

Orff knew only the emended text, and has, one senses, some difficulty in setting the hypermetrical words.

The final rare genre in the codex is the *Tanzlied*, dance-song or carol. *CB* 167a is also set by Orff:

> Swaz hie gat umbe
> daz sint alle^z megede:
> die wellent an man
> alle[n] disen sumer gan.

(Those cavorting round and round here, / they're all maidens: / they want to go without a man / for the whole of this summer.)

The correction this time appears to be that of the scribe h^2 himself, changing the sense from 'all the maidens' to 'all the summer'. Possibly the song led into a dance, a technique attested in the lyrics of Neidhart and still alive in the British folk tradition. The dance in question seems to be an all-girl affair, reminiscent of *Tess of the d'Urbervilles*. The vivid statement of the girls' desire to remain virgin has a robustness all of its own; it seems a long way away from the ethos of courtly love.

CB 172a is a male counter-statement in monostrophic form, again thematically unusual, in that the lover emphasizes his desire to dress up to impress female admirers:

---

[24] The emendations are described in *Carmina Burana* I, 1: *Die moralisch-satirischen Dichtungen*, edited by Alfons Hilka and Otto Schumann (Heidelberg: Carl Winter, 1930), p. 247; see also Cyril Edwards, 'The Magnanimous Sex-Object: Richard the Lionheart in the Medieval German Lyric', in *Courtly Literature: Culture and Context. Proceedings of the 5th triennial Congress of the International Courtly Literature Society, Dalfsen, The Netherlands, 9-16 August 1986*, edited by Keith Busby and Erik Kooper (Amsterdam: John Benjamins, 1990), pp. 159-177; Martin H. Jones, 'Richard the Lionheart in German Literature of the Middle Ages', in *Richard Coeur de Lion in History and Myth*, edited by Janet L. Nelson, King's College London Medieval Studies, VII (London: King's College London Centre for Late Antique and Medieval Studies, 1992), pp. 70-116.

> Ich han eine senede not   div tût mir also we:
> daz machet mir ein winter chalt   vnde ouch der wise sne.
> chome mir div sumerzit,
> so wolde ich prisen minen lip
> um^be ein vil harte schôniz wip.

(I languish in misery which hurts me so much: / a cold winter imposes
this upon me and the white snow, too. / Come summer time / I would
adorn myself / for the sake of a most beautiful woman.)

Only four of the *anonyma* have found their way into the latest edition
of the standard anthology, *Des Minnesangs Frühling*.[25] This itself marks
an advance; the first edition included only two strophes. Why should
this be the case? The earliest named poets of the 'Danubian' school,
Der von Kürenberg, Dietmar von Eist, and Meinloh von Sevelingen,
cultivated the monostrophic form; they also composed woman's voice
lyrics. One problem is that we cannot be certain that the monostrophes
in the *Codex Buranus* are not parts of longer lyrics. However, the
combination of the *Langzeile*, characteristic of genres that were
cultivated at an early stage in the evolution of the lyric, and
monostrophic form suggests that we are justified in regarding many of
the songs in the codex as fortunate survivals of twelfth-century lyric.

Finally, among the most neglected of the treasures contained in the
manuscript are those lyrics which mark a bridge between Latin and the
vernacular, the macaronic, bilingual or polylingual texts. The language
mix in the codex is of varying character and dimensions. In the section
of the manuscript devoted to drinking and gambling songs ('Trink- und
Spielerlieder') it ranges from single German words in predominantly
Latin lyrics (*CB* 225 'schillink') to German refrains, as in *CB* 204, where
Old French 'per dulzor' ('by (your) favour') precedes 'Her wirt, tragent
her nû win / vrolich suln wiur bi dem sin'. ('Mine host, bring wine here;
that it is which gives us good cheer!') German refrains also follow Latin

---

[25] *Des Minnesangs Frühling*, edited by Karl Lachmann, Moriz Haupt, Friedrich
Vogt and Carl von Kraus, revised by Hugo Moser and Helmut Tervooren, 38th
edition (Stuttgart: Hirzel, 1988), 'Namenlose Lieder', nos. VI, VII, IX; IX consists
of two discrete strophes.

love-songs, as in *CB* 180: 'Manda liet, manda liet, / min geselle chŏmet niet.' ('Manda song, Manda song, / my lover is not coming.')

A number of the lyrics move more deliberately towards a blend of two (or more) languages. *CB* 149 *Floret silva nobilis*, a woman's voice lyric set by Orff, has one Latin strophe with a macaronic Latin-German refrain: 'Floret silva undique, / nah mime gesellen ist mir we' ('The forest blooms everywhere, / I miss my lover'), followed by a Middle High German strophe. *CB* 218 *Audientes audiant*, an attack on miserly clerics and lords, alternates Latin and German lines in its first three strophes; the third, however, ends in a line of Old French. The fourth strophe has two lines of Latin followed by two of German, then reverts to the alternating line pattern.

Three of the macaronic lyrics are *pastourelles*, a genre in which the codex is particularly rich. One of these is *CB* 177 *Stetit puella*. The Latin strophes are set by Orff, but not its third, Latin-German strophe. The two other macaronic *pastourelles* occur towards the end of the love-lyric section of the manuscript, followed directly by a Latin poem, *CB* 186 *Svscipe, flos, florem*, which also focuses on the central motif of the *pastourelle*, *deflorare*, and is illustrated by an appropriate miniature.[26] *CB* 184 *Virgo quedam nobilis*, an encounter between a handsome youth and a virgin picking broom, combines German and Latin lines in an unsystematic way. The most harmonious blend of Latin and German is to be found in *CB* 185 *Ich was ein chint so wolgetan*. Here the perfect symmetry of alternating German and Latin lines, followed by a Latin refrain, almost succeeds in masking the complex psychology of the lyric. The narrative purports to be in the female voice, but the point of view fluctuates between that of the voyeuristic male poet and the innocent victim of the seduction. The melody suggested by Korth, Clemencic, and Müller is borrowed from a Latin student song in a late-thirteenth-century manuscript from Florence (Firenze, Laur. Plut. 29,1), *Ecce tempus gaudi*:[27]

---

[26] See pl. 10.
[27] *Carmina Burana. Lateinisch-deutsch*, edited by Korth et al., p. 184.

Ich was ein chint so wolgetan,
uirgo dum florebam.
do brist mich div werlt al.
omnibus placebam.
Refl. Hoy et oe
maledicantur thylie
iuxta uiam posite.

Ia wolde ih an die wisen gan
flores adunare.
do wolde mich ein ungetan
ibi deflorare.

Er nam mich bi der wizen hant,
sed non indecenter.
er wist mich div wise lanch
valde fraudulenter.

Er graif mir an daz wize gewant
valde indecenter.
er fůrte mih bi der hant
multum violenter.

Er sprach: 'vrowe gewir baz,
nemus est remotum.'
dirre wech der habe haz!
planxi et hoc totum.

'Iz stat ein linde wolgetan
non procul auia.
da hab ich mine herphe lan,
timpanum cum lyra.'

Do er zů der linden chom,
dixiᵗ: 'sedeamus.'
div minne twanch sere den man.
'ludum faciamus.'

I was a maid so fair,
a virgin then I flourished.
Then the whole world praised me.
I was pleasing to everyone.
Refrain: Hoy and oy
a curse upon the lime trees
placed next to the road!

I wanted to go to the meadow
to pick flowers.
Then a monster wanted
to deflower me there.

He took me by the white hand,
but not indecently.
He led me along the meadow
most cunningly.

He seized my white dress
most indecently.
He led me by the hand
most violently.

He said: 'Lady, let's go further,
the place is remote.'
A curse upon this path!
I lamented the whole business.

'There is a fair lime tree
not far from the road.
There I have left my harp,
my drum and my lyre.'

When he came to the lime tree,
he said: 'Let us sit down.'
Love oppressed the man sorely.
'Let us play a game.'

Er graif mir an den wizen lip
non absque timore.
er sprah: 'ih mache dich ein wip,
dulcis es cum ore.'

Er warf mir ůf daz hemdelin,
corpore detecta.
er rante mir in daz purgelin
cuspide erecta.

Ernam den chocher unde den bogen,
bene uenabatur!
der selbe hete mich betrogen—
ludus compleatur.

He grasped my white body
not without timidity.
He said: 'I'll make you a woman,
you have a sweet face.'

He threw my little shift open,
uncovered my body.
He charged into my little citadel
with erect spear.

He took his quiver and bow,
well did he hunt!
That same man deceived me—
Let the game be at an end!

APPENDIX

An Index to the German Material in the *Codex Buranus*.[28]

Folio	CB No.	Incipit/Title	Genre
14r	48a	*Hȯrstu friunt den wahter an der cinne* Otto von Botenlauben (MS A: Niune)	alba
56r	133	*Nomina avium*	German interlinear glosses
56r	134	*De nominibus Ferarum*	German interlinear glosses
56v	135a	*Der stȧche winder hat uns uerlan*	summer song
56v	136a	*Solde ih noch den tac geleben*	courtly love lyric
57r	137a	*Springerwir den reg̊en*	dance-song
57r	138a	*In liehter varwe stat der walt*	summer song
57v	139a	*Zergangen ist der winder chalt*	summer song
58r	140a	*Nu sů̇ln wir alle frȯde han*	summer song
58v	141a	*Div heide grů̇net vnde der walt*	summer song
59r	142a	*Ich solde eines morgenes gan*	pastourelle
59r	143a	*Ze ṅwen vrȯden stat min mů̇t* Reinmar, *MF* 203,10	woman's voice lyric
59v	144a	*Ich han gesehen, daz mir in dem* *herçen sanfte tů̇t*	summer song
60r	145a	*Uvẹre diu werlt alle min*	woman's voice lyric
60r	146a	*Nahtegel sing einen don mit sinne*	courtly love lyric
60v	147a	*Sage, dazs ih dirs iemmer lone* Reinmar, *MF* 177,10	messenger song
60v	148a	*Nu sin stolz vnde hovisch* *Venus schiuzet iren bolz*	two strophes (?) of a courtly love lyric
60v	149	*Floret silva nobilis* Macaronic refrain: 'Floret silva undique / nah mime gesellen ist mir we'; German second strophe: 'Grů̇net der walt allenthalben'	woman's voice lyric
61r	150a	*Ich pin keiser ane chrone* Heinrich von Morungen, *MF* 142,19	courtly love lyric
61v	151a	*So wol dir meie, wie du scheidest* Walther von der Vogelweide, L. 51,29	courtly love lyric

---

[28] This catalogue is based on that of Ulrich Müller, 'Mehrsprachigkeit', pp. 88-91, but attempts to be more comprehensive in that it also considers genres other than the lyrics. The *CB* numbers refer to the edition by Hilka/Schumann. Note further abbreviations used: *FB = Fragmenta Burana*; L = Lachmann edition of Walther von der Vogelweide; *MF = Minnesangs Frühling*.

61*v*	152a	*Ich gesach den sumer nie*	summer song
62*r*	153a	*Vrowe, ih pin dir undertan*	courtly love lyric
62*v*	155a	*Si ist schŏner den uro^{we} dido was*	courtly love lyric
65*r*	161a	*Diu werlt froͮt sih uber al*	summer song
65*v*	162a	*Sv̊ziv vrŏwe min*	courtly love lyric
66*r*	163a	*Eine wunecliche stat*	pastourelle
66*v*	164a	*Ih wolde gerne singen*	courtly love lyric
67*r*	165a	*Mir ist ein wip sere in min gemůte chomen*	courtly love lyric
67*r*	166a	*Solde auer ich mit sorgen iemmer leben* Reinmar, *MF* 185,27	courtly love lyric
67*v*	167a	*Swaz hie gat umbe*	dance-song
68*r*	168a	*Nu grv̊net auer div heide* Neidhart von Reuental, *Sommerlied* 11	crusading song
68*r*	169a	*Roter munt, wie du dich swachest* Walther von der Vogelweide, L. 51,37	courtly love lyric
68*v*	170a	*Min vrowe uenus est so gůt*	courtly love lyric
68*v*	171a	*Vroweⁿ wesent vro*	summer song
69*r*	172a	*Ich han eine senede not*	winter song, male voice
69*r*	173a	*Wol ir libe, div so schone*	courtly love lyric
69*v*	174a	*Chume, chume geselle min* Bistrophic. Second strophe: 'Sůzer roservarwer munt'	woman's voice lyric
69*v*	175a	*Taugen minne div ist gůt*	courtly love lyric
70*r*	177	*Stetit puella* Third strophe Latin-German	macaronic pastourelle
70*r-v*	178a	*Ich wil den sumer gruzen*	summer song
70*v*	179a	*Einen brief ich sande einer vrowen gůt* Refrain: 'Selich wip, vil sůzih wip [...]'	courtly love lyric
71*r*	180	*O mi dilectissima* German refrain: 'Manda liet! manda liet! / min geselle chŏmet niet!'	Latin love-lyric
71*r*	180a	*Ich wil truren varen lan* Bistrophic, with refrain. Second strophe: 'Sůziu minne, raine min'. Refrain: 'Ich sage dir, ih sage dir, / min geselle, chum mit mir!'	woman's voice lyric
71*v*	181a	*Der winder zeiget sine chraft* Bistrophic, with refrain. Second strophe: 'Die uogele swigent gegen der zit.' Refrain: 'Wve tůt in rife vnde ouch der sne [...]'	winter song
71*v*	182a	*Vns chumet ein liehte sumerzit* Refrain: 'Swer nah frovden weruen wil [...]'	summer song

72r	183a	*Ich sich den morgen sterne brehen*	alba
72r	184	*Virgo quedam nobilis*	macaronic pastourelle
72r-v	185	*Ich was ein chint so wolgetan*	macaronic pastourelle
81r	112a	*Div mich singen tůt*	courtly love lyric
81v	113a	*Vvaz ist fůr daz senen gůt* Dietmar von Eist, *MF* 32,1	Wechsel
81v	114a	*Der alder werlt ein meister si*	courtly love lyric
82r	115a	*Edile^v vrowe min* Refrain: 'Nach dir ist mir not [...]'	courtly love lyric
87v	195	*Si quis Deciorum* Strophe 7: 'Schuch!'; strophe 13a: 'wir enahten niht uf den Rin'	drinking song
90v	203a	*Vns seit von lutringen Helfrich* Strophe 69 of *Eckenlied*	Dietrich epic
90v	204	*Urbs salue regia* Refrain: 'Her wirt tragent her nů win [...]'	drinking song
92v	211a	*Nu lebe ich mir alrest werde* Walther von der Vogelweide, L.14,38	crusading song
95r	218	*Audientes audiant*	macaronic political lyric
97v	222	*Ego sum abbas* German exclamation: 'wafna wafna!'	drinking song
98r	225	*De Sacerdotibus* One MHG word: 'schillink'	begging song
54v	2*	*Ich lob die liben frǒwen min* Tristrophic. Second strophe: 'Ir roter rosenvarwer mvnt [...].' Third strophe: 'Min leben stat in ir gewalt [...].'	courtly love lyric
FB 5r-6v	15*	*Ludus immo exemplum Dominice resurrectionis* German words in soldiers' song: 'schǎwe'; 'shaẘe alumbe!'	Easter play
107v -111r	16*	*Benediktbeurer Passionsspiel* German in the mouth of Maria Magdalena ('Chramer gip die varwe mier'), the *mercator*, the Virgin Mary, Longinus.	passion play
110v	17*	*Diu mukke mǔz sich sere mǔn* Lines from Freidank's *Bescheidenheit*	aphorisms
112v	23*	*Cantus Ioseph ab Arimathia* Joseph: 'Iesus von gǒtlicher art [...].' Pilate: 'Swer redelicher dinge gert [...].'	passion play
FB 1r	7*	*In anegenge was ein wort*	translation of John 1.1-14

EARTHLY DELIGHTS: THE PICTORIAL IMAGES OF THE *CARMINA BURANA* MANUSCRIPT

Julia Walworth

The manuscript of the *Carmina Burana* contains eight pen-and-ink drawings in spaces provided by the scribe in the text column. The presence of illustrations is evidence of the value placed on this collection of texts by the patron for whom it was made, since miniatures or any kind of figural images in manuscripts of lyric poetry are highly unusual. Surviving collections of medieval Latin lyric generally have little in the way of decoration. Manuscripts of classical Latin lyric were occasionally accompanied by more or less elaborate author portraits ranging from historiated initials to, more rarely, full-page miniatures at the opening of the book or of sections. Figural decoration relating to the content of classical non-epic poems was also an exception rather than the rule.

Surviving illustrated manuscripts of medieval vernacular lyric poetry from the second half of the thirteenth century emphasize the role of the poet as author, performer (as in the Italian troubadour manuscripts), or protagonist, and at times the genres of author portrait and illustrative vignette merge, as in the well-known Manesse Codex. Authorship, or attributed authorship, also determined the organization of these manuscripts, as poems are grouped by poet. In the *Codex Buranus*, however, the poems are grouped by themes, and no poets' names are mentioned. The images relate to the themes of the songs, and often are placed towards the end of the relevant group. With regard to its organization—the arrangement of texts and images—the *Codex Buranus* thus appears to have neither followed nor initiated a tradition.

A look at the individual miniatures, in the order in which they once would have appeared, before some leaves were lost and the gatherings of the manuscript were re-arranged, reveals that they function more as an enriching complement to the groups of songs than as mere illustrative visualization of particular texts.

The image most frequently associated with the *Carmina Burana*, and also the most frequently reproduced, is the picture of Fortuna and her wheel that now appears at the very beginning of the manuscript [pl. 1]. Originally it would have been immediately preceded by several leaves (now folios 43 to 48) of poems concerning the fickle nature of Fortuna. The concept of Fortuna's wheel is found in the sixth-century *Consolation of Philosophy* of Boethius (Book Two, Prose Two): 'I spin my wheel and find pleasure in raising the low to a high place and lowering those who were on top.'[1] By the twelfth and thirteenth centuries, variations and elaborations on the Boethian image could be found in both texts and pictorial representations, and it was therefore a concept probably familiar to most educated people. Several of the poems in the *Codex Buranus* refer to Fortuna's wheel (e.g. *CB* 16, 3, 1-3: 'Fortune rota uoluitur: descendo minoratus, / alter in altum tollitur; nimis exaltatus rex sedet in uertice [...]': 'The wheel of fortune turns; powerless I descend, / another is carried upwards; exalted on high the king sits at the top [...]').

The earliest surviving visual representation of Fortuna's wheel is found in an eleventh-century compilation of computistical and mathematical texts from the abbey of Montecassino (Archivio dell'Abbazio, MS 189, p. 146 (*sic*).[2] Although Fortuna herself is not depicted here, other features found in the *Codex Buranus* image and in many later examples are present. Four men on the edge of the wheel represent the instability of good fortune: at the top of the wheel a crowned ruler appears to be immovable, while to the right a king (possibly the same king) struggles to maintain a grip on the turning wheel as his fine clothes fall away; a nearly naked man is crushed under the wheel, and finally at the left a young (?) man pulls himself upwards, being carried towards the top by the motion of the wheel.

---

[1]   Boethius, *The Consolation of Philosophy*, translated, with introduction and notes by Richard Green (Indianapolis: Bobbs-Merrill Educational Publishing, 1962), p. 24.
[2]   Pierre Courcelle, *La Consolation de philosophie dans la tradition littéraire: antécédents et postérité de Boèce* (Paris: Études Augustiniennes, 1976), pl. 65.

The interior of the wheel is divided into two halves, the top inscribed 'Prosperitas', the bottom 'Adversitas'. Latin *tituli* (in a different hand from the other text on the folio) identify the 'state' of each of the figures: 'Regno (I reign), Regnavi (I have reigned), Sum sine regno (I am without a kingdom), Regnabo (I will reign)'. These *tituli* frequently accompany depictions of the wheel of fortune and were added, very shortly after the writing of the manuscript, to the *Codex Buranus* miniature as well. As in the Montecassino miniature, the four figures on the wheel in the *Codex Buranus* could be the same man at different stages in his career. A variation on this, in which the four 'states' are exemplified by well-known historical figures, occurs in *CB* 14 and 16.

Depictions of Fortuna with her wheel tend to fall into two broad categories: images in which Fortuna is shown actively turning the wheel from one side–sometimes with a proper crank and axle mechanism; and images in which Fortuna appears at the centre of the wheel— sometimes turning the wheel around her. The *Codex Buranus* miniature belongs to the second category. Here Fortuna is a crowned and richly dressed woman seated and static at the centre of the wheel. An almost contemporary depiction of the wheel of fortune at the opening of a manuscript of Josephus's *On the Jewish Wars* from Scheyern (Munich, Bayerische Staatsbibliothek, Clm 17404, fol. 203v, *c*. 1240s) shows a somewhat similar arrangement [pl. 2]. In this case, the wheel of fortune is part of a larger composition depicting the fall of Jerusalem and linking Fortuna to the actions of the Fates and the natural changes of seasons. At the centre of the concentric circles, however, Fortuna is seated, surrounded by the familiar 'victims' of her power (only three in this instance). Instead of turning the wheel, the Scheyern Fortuna is shown with her left hand removing the crown from the falling man (who is committing suicide) and with her right hand crowning the rising man. While the *Codex Buranus* Fortuna neither grasps the wheel nor actively aids the rise and fall of men, she holds two symmetrically positioned scrolls in her raised hands, the left hand palm-downwards and the right palm-upwards, reflecting the motion of the wheel and good and bad fortune. It is likely that these scrolls were intended to contain inscriptions, perhaps relating to good and bad fortune.

Seated frontally, with arms symmetrically raised holding extended scrolls, the *Codex Buranus* Fortuna strongly resembles twelfth- and thirteenth-century allegorical figures of Sapientia or Philosophia [pl. 3]. As the largest of all the figures in the miniature, Fortuna is also reminiscent of images of Christ or of temporal rulers, and although her power may be limited to the terrestrial, this Fortuna is undoubtedly an ineluctable force. As some of the songs and verses in the manuscript make clear, fortune's capricious and mutable character is itself as unchanging as a natural force.

The next miniature (now folio 77*v* [pl. 4]) is the only narrative miniature in the manuscript and depicts the tragic end of the love between Dido and Aeneas from the fourth book of Virgil's *Aeneid*. Several scenes are shown on each of the two horizontal registers separated and surrounded by a wide frame. At the top left Aeneas bids farewell to Dido, in the middle Dido appears to be looking over the ramparts talking to two women (one of them her sister?), while at the right, but actually occupying the greater part of the space, Dido leaps to her death from the palace wall onto a pyre in the courtyard below, thrusting a sword into her heart. In the lower register Aeneas is shown several times: on the shore; in a small boat travelling to his ship; and finally in the forecastle of the ship as it sails away. Although the two registers depict different moments, the composition of the whole is such that Dido appears to be looking down from her palace to the ship below, while Aeneas appears to be looking up from his ship to the dramatic suicide of Dido above.

The story of Dido and Aeneas would have been very familiar to contemporary readers of the *Codex Buranus*, both from Latin school texts and from well-known vernacular accounts, such as Heinrich von Veldeke's *Eneit*. By the twelfth and thirteenth centuries, this tale of tragic love was the subject of poems and songs and had a life of its own independent of longer narratives. Several of these texts are included in the *Codex Buranus*, along with poems dealing with the fall of Troy. The *Aeneid* was not commonly illustrated in the Middle Ages, and there was no standard iconographic cycle from which the *Codex Buranus* artist could select. The *Codex Buranus* illustration reveals some similarities, however, with both Late Antique and more contemporary depictions of the death of Dido. The image of Dido watching in despair from a high window as Aeneas's ship sails away occurs in the fifth-century Vatican Virgil (Vatican, Biblioteca Apostolica, Cod. lat. 3225, fol. 39*v* [pl. 5]), while the early-thirteenth-century illustrated manuscript of the *Eneit* (Berlin, Staatsbibliothek, Preußischer Kulturbesitz, Ms. germ. fol. 282, fol. 17*v* [pl. 6]) shows Dido falling onto her sword from a height. There is no reason for linking the production of the *Eneit* manuscript and the *Codex Buranus*, so it seems probable that these two almost contemporary depictions of Dido leaping or falling onto the pyre are evidence of a common pictorial tradition. Certainly, late-thirteenth-century French manuscripts of the historical compilation *Histoire ancienne jusqu'à César*, in which the death of Dido was frequently illustrated, bring together the high tower, the departure of Aeneas's ship and Dido's suicide in a manner reminiscent of the *Codex Buranus* miniature [pl. 7].

In the context of the *Codex Buranus*, the image of Dido falling from the tower may have brought to mind the king falling from the wheel of fortune. Together with the songs dealing with Troy, which occur in the same section of the manuscript, the miniature of Dido and Aeneas provides a vivid example of the actions of Fortune in the world and of the power of love. The overall impression created by the poems and the miniature, however, is more that of unavoidable tragedy than of admonition against placing too much importance on temporal success and happiness.

The only full-page miniature in the *Codex Buranus*, and one of the most unusual, is found on folio 64*v* [pl. 8], although originally the Dido miniature would have preceded it. Like the Dido miniature, the pictorial space is divided into two registers, but instead of a narrative, each register contains a forest scene: that on top populated primarily by birds, that on the bottom populated primarily by animals (a rabbit, horse, stag, fox, and lion). This miniature has sometimes been referred to as the first landscape in Western post-classical art, and while such claims may be anachronistic, it is difficult to find similar miniatures in which the natural world appears totally uninhabited by humans or anthropomorphic figures and with such formal framing.

The forest miniature was placed towards the end of a section headed *De Vere* containing songs celebrating springtime, summer, the growth and bounty of the natural world, and erotic love. The miniature cannot be said to 'illustrate' any particular song or verses in a literal way, but efforts of the artist to produce an image of natural profusion are striking and echo the exuberant lines of the poems. A variety of vegetal forms are found in these scenes; some are recognizable elements of contemporary background and forest scenes (e.g. the lime tree), while other plants seem to be components of historiated initials transplanted and gone wild (e.g. the spiralling leafy plants in the lower register).

Although similar 'landscape' illustrations have not been found, inspiration for this miniature may have come from a number of sources. The stylized forms in historiated initials have been mentioned. Creation cycles frequently depict a variety of animals and plants together, either as an illustration of the fifth or sixth day, or of Adam naming the animals. Bestiaries also sometimes depict animals in a natural setting, and both animals and plant forms (stylized and more natural) are found in the early-thirteenth-century artist's pattern book now in Vienna (Vienna, Österreichische Nationalbibliothek, Cod. 507, fol. 10v [pl. 9]). All of the elements of these images are frequently found in contemporary manuscript illumination, but their use in the *Codex Buranus* is remarkable. The fantastic flowers, vines, swaying trees, and the profusion of birds and animals are reminiscent of many of the images used in the spring love-songs in the *Carmina Burana*, while the great number of birds in the top register and the animals in the bottom suggest that there may be links also to the naming poems (*CB* 133 and 134).

The next miniature (fol. 72v [pl. 10]) depicts more directly the love between beautiful young men and women that is the subject of the preceding series of songs and verses. In this picture, a relatively early use in a manuscript of the type of imagery associated with courtly love, a well-dressed young man offers some flowers to his lover. The two types of flowers shown—lilies and roses (?)—also are frequently named in love poetry. It is the only miniature in the manuscript to be placed within the text of a poem (*CB* 186) and is particularly closely linked to the poem, in which the poet plays on the word 'flower' as signifying both natural flowers and the beloved, appropriately named Flora.

The opening line of the poem, 'Svscipe, flos, florem, quia flos designat amorem!' ('Flower, take this flower, since the flower signifies love!'), could function as a caption for the picture positioned just below it on the page. Similarly, the last two lines of the poem (simultaneously the final lines of the section of love-songs in the manuscript) comprise a Latin tag dealing with the dichotomy between image and reality: 'Flos in pictura non est flos, immo figura; / Qui pingit florem, non pingit floris odorem.' ('A flower in a picture is not a flower, but only an image of a flower. He who paints a flower, cannot paint its scent.') The reader is thus led back to consideration of the painted image on the page. Just as the 'flower' which the poet offers to his beloved may be the poem, it is possible that the contrast between the natural flower and the painted image may also allude to the contrast between the experience of love and verses about it.

While the first four miniatures occur at fairly wide intervals at the end of groups of texts, the last four miniatures are distributed over just four folios and are also quite closely linked thematically to the themes of the poems – drinking and gaming.

A group of men is shown drinking on folio 89v [pl. 11], the miniature set appropriately just above the first line of a song (*CB* 202) beginning 'Potatores exquisiti'. At the far right, a man raises his cup and blesses it in imitation of a priest blessing a chalice—the sort of irreverent allusion found in many of the songs as well. On folio 91r [pl. 12] two groups of men are gathered around tables, gambling with dice while being served drinks. Once again, the first line of the song following the miniature (*CB* 207) provides a fitting caption: 'Tessera, blandita fueras michi, quando tenebam.' ('Dice, you were sweet to me, so long as I was holding you.') Finally, on facing leaves (folios 91v and 92r [pls 13 and 14]) two further games are shown. Two men seated on comfortable benches play some form of backgammon on folio 91v, while on folio 92r a similar depiction of a chess game in progress is positioned between two poems dealing with the game and with the moves allowed to the various pieces.

While the chess and backgammon players in the *Codex Buranus* miniatures appear appropriately wealthy (they sit on relatively elaborate benches with cushions, and a servant is in attendance), the depiction of the dice players is more sedate than most such scenes, written or pictorial. The thirteenth-century didactic poem *Der Welsche Gast* by Thomasin von Zerklaere denounces dice as leading to uncontrolled anger and violence, and one of the illustrations in this work shows a desperate man who has lost all his clothes (Heidelberg, Universitätsbibliothek, Cod. pal. germ. 389, fol. 62*r* [pl. 15]). The rapidity with which one could lose everything was a feature of dice games frequently noted in medieval accounts, and this is a theme found in the *Codex Buranus* songs as well: 'Tessera deponit hominem summe rationis. / Sunt comites ludi mendacia, iurgia, nudi, / Rara fides, furta, macies, substantia curta.' ('Dice bring down even the most rational man. / The companions of the game are lies, quarrels, nakedness, / disloyalty, theft, hunger, loss of wealth', *CB* 207, II,2-III,2.)

Backgammon or tables, as it was called because of the board on which these games were played, is not specifically mentioned in the *Codex Buranus* texts. Various versions of backgammon were popular, however, and it was frequently included along with dice and chess in medieval treatises on games. By the thirteenth century, dice, backgammon, and chess had come to be ranked in a sort of hierarchy, with dice being the lowest and chess being the highest. The connotations of the three games are neatly exemplified in a story included at the beginning of the Book of Games (*Libro del Acedrex*) written by King Alfonso X of Castile in 1283 and surviving in a sumptuously illustrated manuscript produced not much later (Escorial, Cod. T.I.6). As an explanation of the origins of different types of games, a story is told of an Indian king and his three wise men. The wise men differed in their views, and each brought forward a game to exemplify his approach. One man brought chess, because in this game skill, experience, and the use of reason determine the winner. Another brought dice in order to prove that reason and skill are of no importance when it comes to good or bad fortune—only luck determines fate. The third brought backgammon, showing that, with skill, one could lessen the adverse consequences of a bad throw of the dice. Backgammon was probably included in the *Codex Buranus* because it belonged with dice and chess in any general account of games and gambling. It is even possible that the artist was familiar with an illustrated treatise on games, though an obvious source is not known.

With the chess illustration, the miniatures in the *Codex Buranus* come to an end. For whatever reason, the religious plays were not illustrated (or no illustrations have survived). No other works by the artist have yet been identified, though one can assume from the quality of the drawing that he (or she) was an experienced artist. It is unlikely that the sources of the texts in the *Codex Buranus* were illustrated, so the artist would have made use of appropriate pictorial traditions, as suggested in several cases above. Stylistically related manuscripts or works have not yet been found, and more art-historical research is needed before one can assess whether the style of the miniatures might contribute to the debate on the place of origin of the manuscript. In general terms, the miniatures support the dating of the text of the manuscript to the second quarter of the thirteenth century, and they certainly fit generally into the context of the south of the German-speaking region. Pen-drawing on a coloured ground was a popular technique in south German illumination, and it is perhaps no coincidence that the earliest surviving examples of illustrations of secular vernacular narratives, the Rodenegg Iwein wallpaintings or the romance manuscripts now in Berlin and Munich, were also made in the south (cf. folio 30*r* from the Munich *Tristan* [pl. 16]).

The inclusion of the miniatures appears to have been part of the original conception of the manuscript; the scribe left space for them, and thought was clearly given to coordinating the subject of the miniatures with the immediately surrounding texts as well as with the general theme of a particular group. Similarly, the large initials decorated with faces suit the overall character of a manuscript that was unusually elaborate for its contents. The placement of the miniatures, however, usually towards the end of the relevant group of texts, suggests some uncertainty about the production. A convincing explanation of the unusual placement of the miniatures is proposed by

Peter and Dorothee Diemer in their commentary in Vollmann's 1987 edition of the *Carmina Burana*:[3] the scribe allocated space for a miniature when he was coming to the end of a particular group of texts and could see that space would be available, often on the verso of a folio or, in at least two cases (the forest and the pair of lovers), at the end of a gathering.

Like the texts, the miniatures draw on established traditions, often using imagery related to that used in the texts but without being directly dependent on the texts. These pictorial images would have been familiar to the clerical and formally educated audience by and for whom the majority of these poems and songs were written. It is noteworthy that, in a manuscript in which secular subjects were chosen for illustration (at least as the manuscript appears today), there are none of the images relating to or suggestive of combat or hunting, so beloved of the secular aristocracy of the thirteenth century and so frequently found in their books and decorating their belongings.

It is by no means clear, and perhaps unlikely, that there was a systematic overall programme dictating the selection of subjects for illustration. The poems themselves manifest a variety of themes and attitudes, from religious to bawdy, from bitter satire and moralizing to delight in the beauty and pleasures of the world. The pictures likewise relate more to the groups of poems they accompany than to each other. One might initially wonder whether the illustration of both the wheel of fortune and the death of Dido was not intended to convey a moralizing message about the insecurity of worldly happiness, as indeed there is an undoubted resonance between the two themes. However, the miniature in the *Codex Buranus* does not present Dido as a negative exemplum; the manner in which the death of Dido is depicted, with Aeneas as witness, places more emphasis on the tragic aspect of their love. In a somewhat similar manner, the miniatures of the dice and chess players are relatively neutral and do

---

[3] *Carmina Burana*: *Texte und Übersetzungen*, edited by Benedikt Konrad Vollmann, Bibliothek des Mittelalters, 13 (Frankfurt am Main: Deutscher Klassiker Verlag, 1987), pp. 1289-98.

not exploit the possible contrasts between the two games. There is no internal evidence in the manuscript to indicate how contemporary readers understood the miniatures, but the drawing of a courtly young woman added in the margin of folio 39*r* at the beginning of the dialogue between Phyllis and Flora at about the turn of the thirteenth to fourteenth centuries suggests that at least one later reader's reception was not of a moralizing nature [pl. 17].

The miniatures are perhaps best understood as visual counterparts of the songs and verses within the relevant groups. In fact, although the miniature of Fortuna is most frequently reproduced in connection with the manuscript, it is the miniature of the forest with its exuberant variety of forms that characterizes this manuscript: a true paradise of poetry, music, and visual images.

SELECTED BIBLIOGRAPHY

Facsimiles

Carmina Burana. Facsimile Reproduction of the Manuscript Clm 4660 and Clm 4660a, edited by Bernhard Bischoff, Publications of Mediaeval Musical Manuscripts, 9 (Brooklyn, N.Y.: Institute of Mediaeval Music, 1967). Also available in a German version: *Carmina Burana. Faksimile-Ausgabe der Handschrift Clm 4660 und 4660a,* edited by Bernhard Bischoff (Munich: Prestel, 1967).

Der Welsche Gast des Thomasîn von Zerclaere: Codex Palatinus Germanicus 389 der Universitätsbibliothek Heidelberg. Commentary by Friedrich Neumann and Ewald Vetter (Wiesbaden: Ludwig Reichert, 1974).

Alfonso X el Sabio: Libros del ajedrez, dados y tablas, 2 vols (Madrid: Patrimonio Nacional, 1987).

Editions and Translations

Alfonso el Sabio: Libros de Acedrex, Dados e Tablas, edited and translated by Arnold Steiger (Geneva: Droz, 1941).

Boethius, *The Consolation of Philosophy,* translated, with introduction and notes by Richard Green (Indianapolis: Bobbs-Merrill Education Publishing, 1962).

Carmina Burana: Texte und Übersetzungen, edited by Benedikt Konrad Vollmann, Bibliothek des Mittelalters, 13 (Frankfurt am Main: Deutscher Klassiker Verlag, 1987).

Further reading

Pierre Courcelle, *La Consolation de philosophie dans la tradition littéraire: antécédents et postérité de Boèce* (Paris: Études Augustiniennes, 1967).

Pierre and Jeanne Courcelle, *Lecteurs païens et lecteurs chrétiens de l'Énéide. 2: les manuscrits illustrés de l'Énéide du Xe au XVe siècle* (Paris: Institut de France, 1984).

Richard Eales, 'The game of chess: an aspect of medieval knightly culture', in *The Ideals and Practice of Medieval Knighood [1]. Papers from the first and second Strawberry Hill conferences,* edited by Christopher Harper-Bill and Ruth Harvey (Woodbridge: Boydell, 1986), pp. 12-34.

Ernst Kitzinger, 'World map and fortune's wheel: a medieval mosaic floor in Turin', *Proceedings of the American Philosophical Society,* CXVII (1973), pp. 344-73.

H.J.R Murray, 'The medieval games of tables', *Medium Aevum* X (1941), pp. 57-69.

Michael Schilling, 'Rota fortunae: Beziehungen zwischen Bild und Text in mittelalterlichen Handschriften', in *Deutsche Literatur des späten Mittelalters. Hamburger Colloquium 1973*, edited by Wolfgang Harms and L. Peter Johnson (Berlin: Schmidt, 1975), pp. 293-313.

Georg Steer, 'Das Fortuna-Bild der "Carmina Burana" – Handschrift Clm 4660. Eine Darstellung der "fortuna caesarea" Kaiser Friedrichs II?', in *Literatur und bildende Kunst im Tiroler Mittelalter,* edited by E. Kühebacher, Innsbrucker Beiträge zur Kulturwissenschaft, Germanistische Reihe, 15 (Innsbruck: Institut für Germanistik der Universität Innsbruck, 1982), pp. 183-207.

LIST OF PLATES

Pl. 12   Munich, Bayerische Staatsbibliothek, Clm 4660, *Codex Buranus*, fol. 91*r*. Gambling with dice (photo: Bayerische Staatsbibliothek, Munich).

Pl. 13   Munich, Bayerische Staatsbibliothek, Clm 4660, *Codex Buranus*, fol. 91*v*. A game of backgammon (photo: Bayerische Staatsbibliothek, Munich).

Pl. 14   Munich, Bayerische Staatsbibliothek, Clm 4660, *Codex Buranus*, fol. 92*r*. A game of chess (photo: Bayerische Staatsbibliothek, Munich).

Pl. 15   Heidelberg, Universitätsbibliothek, Cod. pal. germ. 389, fol. 62*r* (detail). Losing at dice, from Thomasin von Zerklaere, *Der Welsche Gast*, second half of thirteenth century (photo: the Universitätsbibliothek, Heidelberg).

Pl. 16   Munich, Bayerische Staatsbibliothek, Cgm 51, fol. 30*r*. Scenes from the Munich *Tristan*, second quarter of thirteenth century (photo: Bildarchiv Foto Marburg).

Pl. 17   Munich, Bayerische Staatsbibliothek, Clm 4660, *Codex Buranus*, fol. 39*r*. Marginal drawing of a courtly young woman (photo: Bayerische Staatsbibliothek, Munich).

Pl. 18   Munich, Bayerische Staatsbibliothek, Clm 4660, *Codex Buranus*, fol. 56*r*. Glossed birds and beasts (photo: Bayerische Staatsbibliothek, Munich).

Pl. 19   Forschungsbibliothek Gotha, Chart. A 823, fol. 43*r*. The poet Freidank, *c*. 1400 (photo: the Forschungsbibliothek, Gotha).

Pl. 20   Munich, Bayerische Staatsbibliothek, Clm 4660a, *Fragmenta Burana*, fol. 1*r*. A Waldensian text? (photo: Bayerische Staatsbibliothek, Munich)

Pl. 21   Munich, Bayerische Staatsbibliothek, Clm 4660, *Codex Buranus*, fol. 90*v*. *Eckenlied*, strophe 69: a collision between a heroic warrior and an Arthurian hero (photo: Bayerische Staatsbibliothek, Munich).

Pl. 22   Munich, Bayerische Staatsbibliothek, Clm 4660, *Codex Buranus*, fol. 60*r*. Sex-change in the medieval lyric (photo: Bayerische Staatsbibliothek, Munich).

PLATES

Plate 1

Plate 2

Plate 3

E JI Dolor nunc ne solar richiit olea alb nce xpti
inus. Abcecius hugos. despernis petro. exclusis l.in
grico. Uris regius corte renus. quin nec brinus nec est ra
res maximus uideat pringuere inc sut potest souere uel
p ere Cur b urns inuida nocte natas sugia lingua bal
lena opia mea turbos gaudia. ne c c t c

Plate 4

Plate 5

Plate 6

Plate 7

Plate 8

Plate 9

Plate 10

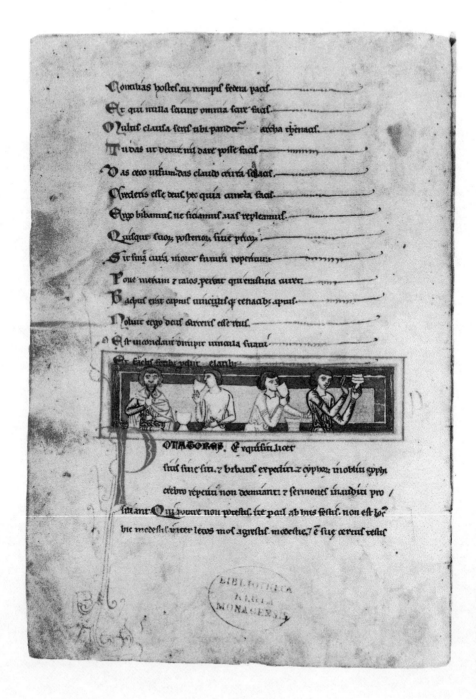

Plate 11

Bachus ad amorem instigat iuniorem. mente rigidiorem. z hic gpeie Hic est locus annualis festumq̈ natalis ubi liberalis est ista regula. Cum ergo saturamus uinum tunc cantamus. te deum laudamus. z hic gpeie Nos qui xpinamus. z uina poreamus. prius non bibamus donec dicamus Bachus est suauis. sur tamen sepe grauis bibentibz incaute hac inmo derite. Prouide non obruitatur. s̃ lauriul bibatur. dign̄ tam nutriatur. z hic gpeie Ergo nos ludamus. sorres piciam. leraurer bibamus z hic gpeie V E R S V S.

Ynaus quando bibit que non sunt debita dicit
Cum bene poeatur que non sunt debita fatur.
Cum bene sum ponis tunc uersib; effluo meis.
Cum sicco sioxe nec in tre nec in hec nec in hoc cor

Tessera blandita fuerat michi quando tenebam.

Plate 12

Tessera psida concaua res mala tessera grandis.

Tessara materies est omnis porcionis.

Tessara deponit hominem summe racionis.

Sunt comitesludi mendacia iurra nudi.

Rara fides iurra macies substancia aurra

Hu res exce canes segnes celeres z inanes

Sunt mea spes quia dant michi res z multiplicat es

Pignora cum nummis cum cassis precia summis.

Veniuntur ve predantur michi sic famulantur.

Littera bis bina me dat uel sillaba trina.

Si mich demarur capud ex reliquo generatur.

Bestia sucenter penuis ero recta decenter.

Da si uereor ero uel sum laicos negz clerio.

Roch pedes miges tener equus miles z rex

Confiebus uecur ex ichus nox maris ad ichus

Vex tonar intrania trahe cost capta velue clama.

Plate 13

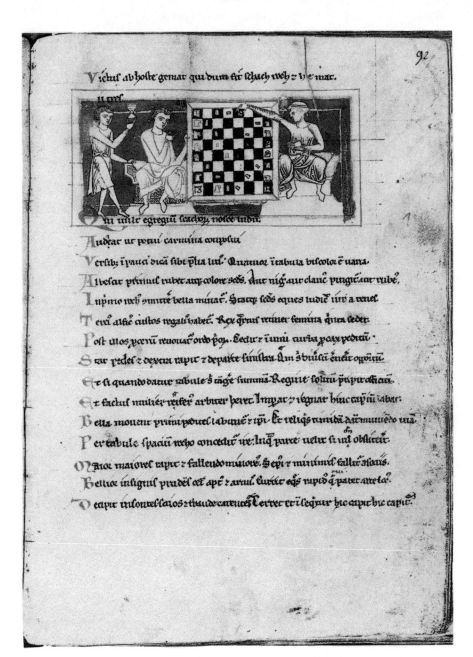

Plate 14

Plate 15

Plate 16

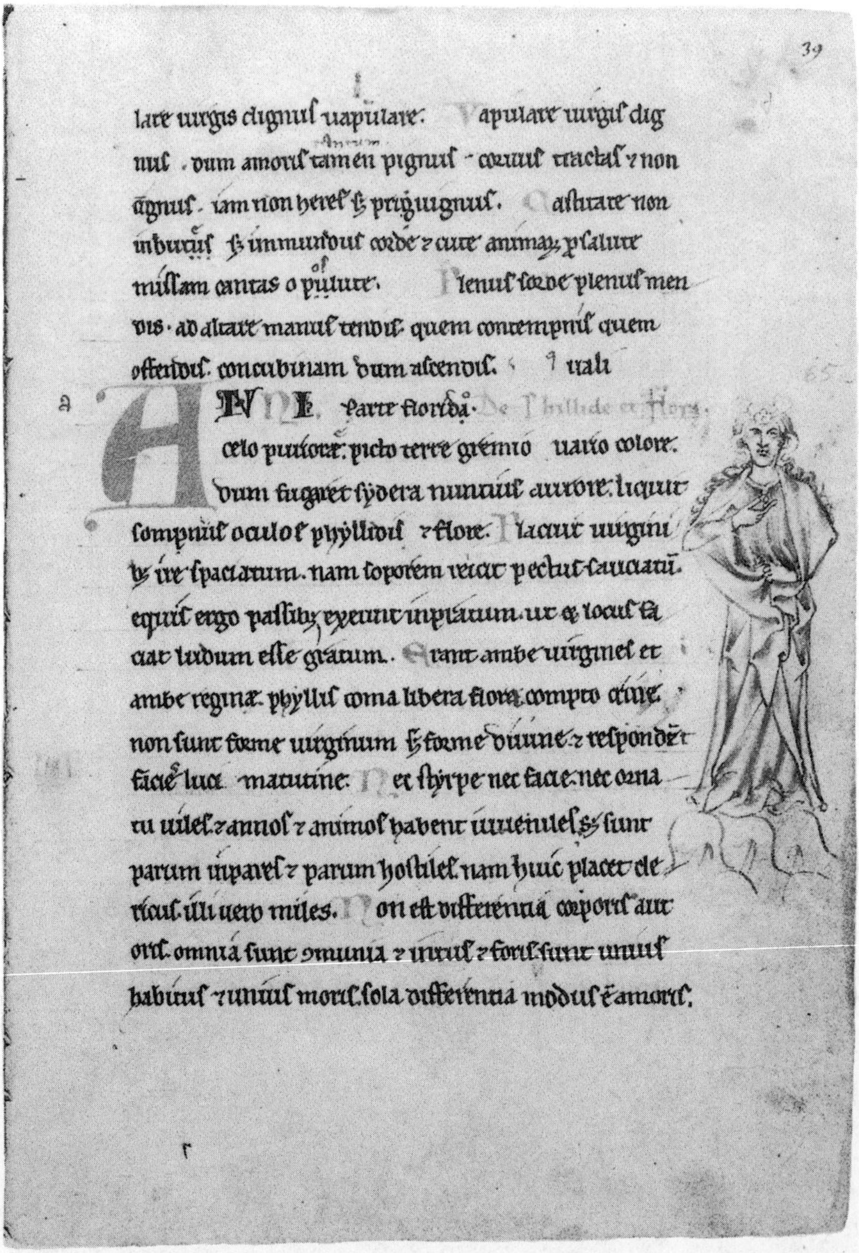

lare uirgis dignus uapulare. Vapulare uirgis dignus. dum amoris tamen pignus · coruus tractas z non
agnus. iam non heres z priuignus. Asturare non
inburis z immundus corde z cute animam psalure
missam cantas o pulure. Plenus corde plenus men-
dis. ad altare manus tendis. quem contempnis quem
offendis. concubinam dum ascendis. Iuali

ANNI parte florida.
celo puriore: picto terre gremio uario colore.
dum fugaret sydera nuntius aurore. liquit
sompnus oculos phyllidis zflore. Placuit uirgini
ly ire spaciatum. nam topotem reuat pectus cruciatum.
equis ergo passibz exeunt inpratum. ut et locus fa-
ciat ludum esse gratum. Erant ambe uirgines et
ambe regine. phyllis coma libera flore compto crine.
non sunt forme uirginum z forme diuine. z respondet
facie luci matutine. Nec stirpe nec facie nec orna-
tu uiles. z annos z animos habent iuueniles z sunt
parum inpares z parum hostiles. nam huic placet cle-
ricus illi uero miles. Non est differentia corporis aut
oris. omnia sunt communia z intus z foris sunt unius
habitus z unius moris. sola differentia modus est amoris.

Plate 17

atq; quadrupedum .quoq; modulamina uincit phenix unica.

Inauius confinio est paucui mansio. sol est inestistio regen

te domicuio.dulsisona resonat harundo florde cum flordet

florent uites pampinis.odorifera surgunt gramina.gaudet

agricola Dunc dracones fluminum.scatent emanantium.

ymber saluberrimus irrigat terra funditus.catharracas reser

tur olimpus.redolent aromata. cum cynamomo balsama.

urtent uiola.rosa z ambrosia.coeunt animalia Noia xiiii.

Ille uolucres celi resera smde f.sh. Tu in dulcisona cape smt le cel philomia.

Accipit nisi cap.atq; ciconia.picul. Lauduia nlla triu fugiat cicedula tactu

Pica metops lar.atq; loafte. ibis. Lne z lucinia cui lualus cape pua

Ardea. ut turt.seu bubo.monedola uult. Versu stare neq; car duelis. sq; recedit.

Iris asst agle pisicul? herodiusq;. De nominib' feraz.

Nata piles h stare coluba. palubes. Noia laucaz. q h socianda feraz

Cezn edax. coruus.upupe ficedula poia. S et leo sit pin q cunctaz hisile?

Noctua. frigellus.seu nisicorax. ama Huic panthera. tigs. connitas cu leopardis.

Ilut in purpx. onociacu? ? ans z orix. Rinocer seu sprendr atq; camel?

Cugn oloz. stn. merg. z deia q; turd? Iruic z ualuos elephares iungo Purses.

Qualisqia. o muia fasian z origomes. Bubal' z pard. uelox nimu q; diomeda.

Gruis z pelhcan pauoq; anas. aluetus. Vrs. ap. ceru aude sumut i esus.

Aurisic. cupide sepiula. epicule q; Hinnul; z capa. capean. simia. spinga

Grica' haut z eru fusari h restebur. Lnre lup atq; lep. uulpis uulpecla me d

S pas z attange muisuaga z strione. Taral. z migale liner. castea. rebeh;

S te ceseu' saihea. e psitae'.atq; cicada. Onis.mustela.sorex. gur glurus. murens.

Te vesp ssko h huiuo n retueto. Cepulo spiriolu. reliq z e ulhn.

Plate 19

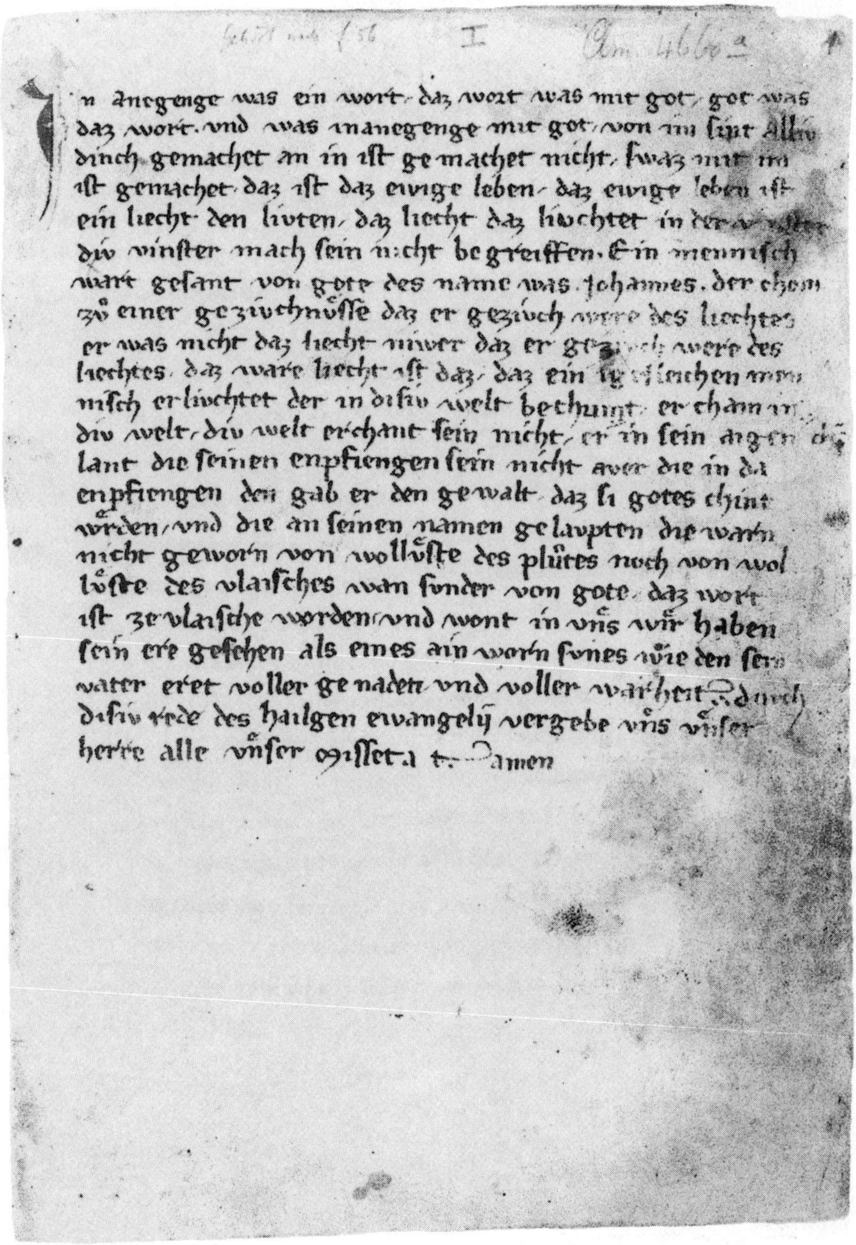
I
Clm. 4660a
In anegenge was ein wort. daz wort was mit got. got was
daz wort. vnd was in anegenge mit got. von im sint allív
dinch gemachet an in ist gemachet nicht. swaz mit im
ist gemachet. daz ist daz ewige leben. daz ewige leben ist
ein liecht den liuten. daz liecht daz liuchtet in der vinster
div vinster mach sein nicht begreiffen. Ein mennisch
wart gesant von gote des name was. Johannes. der chom
zů einer geziuchnússe daz er geziuch were des liechtes
er was nicht daz liecht niwer daz er geziuch were des
liechtes. daz ware liecht ist daz. daz ein iglichen men
nisch erliuchtet der in disiv welt bechumt. er cham in
div welt. div welt erchant sein nicht. er in sein aigen
lant die seinen enpfiengen sein nicht aver die in da
enpfiengen den gab er den gewalt daz si gotes chint
wůrden. vnd die an seinen namen gelaupten die warn
nicht geworn von wollúste des plůtes noch von wol
lúste des vlaisches wan sunder von gote. daz wort
ist ze vlaische worden. vnd wont in vns wir haben
sein ere gesehen als eines ainworn sunes wie den sein
vater eret voller genaden vnd voller warheit. durch
disiv rede des hailgen ewangelÿ vergebe vns vnser
herre alle vnser missetat. amen

Plate 20

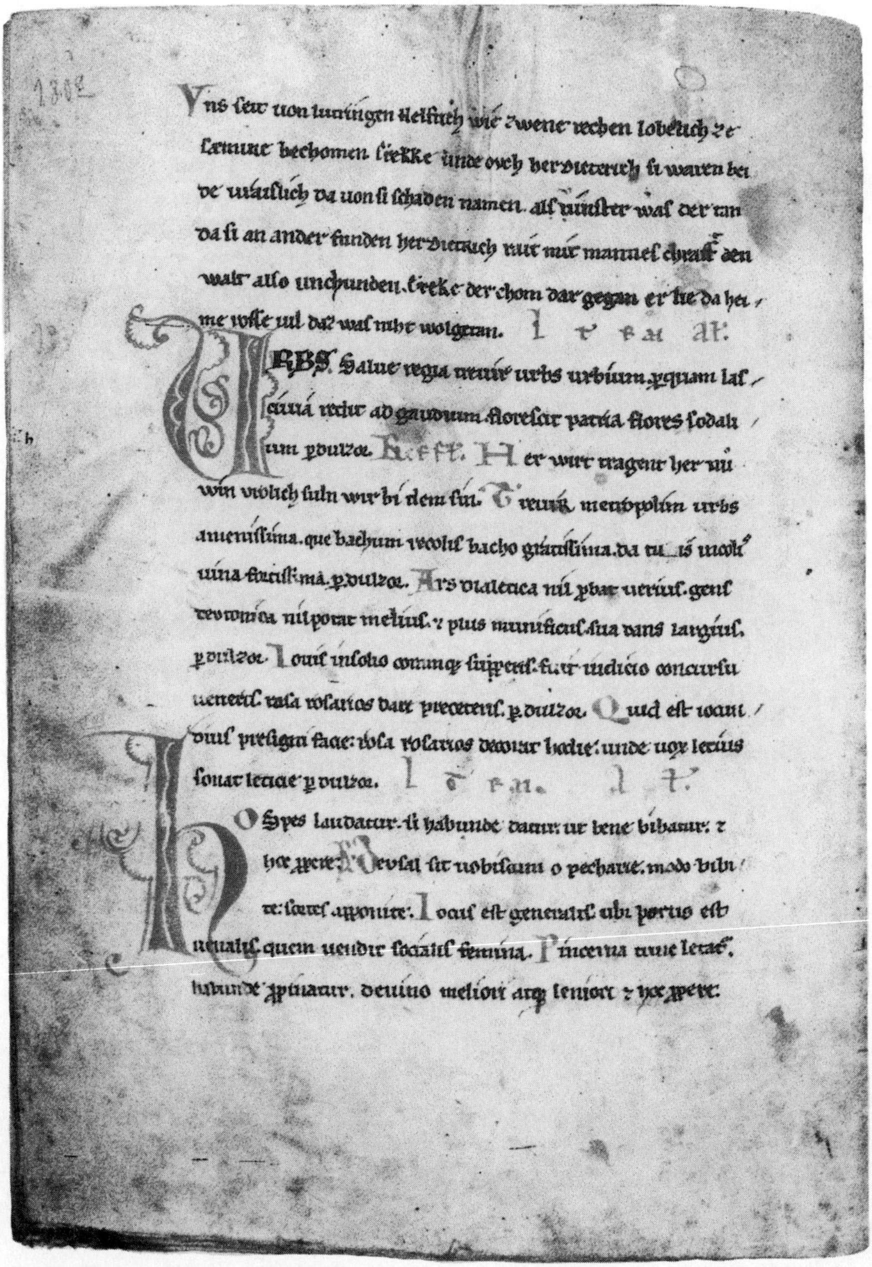

Vns sew von turingen helfrich wie zwene rechen lobeltch ze
semune bechomen krekke vnde ovch herdieterich si waren bei
he vriutlich da von si schaden namen. als vinster was der tan
da si an ander funden her dieterich rut mit mannes chraft den
walt also vnchunden. krekke der chom dar gegan er lie da hei
me wiste vil das was mir wolgetan. Item At:

RBS. Salue regia nenur urbs urbium. y quam las
cinia redit ad gaudium florescit patria flores sodali
um p. dulzok. Keft. Her wur tragent her uu
win vrolich suln wir bi dem sin. Trenta menopolim urbs
amenissima. que bachum recolit bacho gratissima. da tu is mosh
uina suauiss ma. p. dulzok. Ars vialenca nil pbat ueriul. gens
teutonica nil potar melius. y plus munificus sua dans largius.
p. dulzok. Touis insolto comma supent. fiat iudicio concursu
nenenc rata rosarios dare precenis. p. dulzok. Quid est wam
unus prestgin facie: isla rosarios denour hodie: unde uox lecius
sonar lencie p. dulzok. Item. It:

Ospes laudatur. si habunde datur. ut bene bibatur. z
hoc prete: Reusat sit nobiscum o pecharie. modo bibi
re: socus apponitre: Tocus est generalis ubi portus est
neualis. quem uendir socialis femina. Princena tune letas.
habunde ppinatur. denino meliori arz seniori z hoc prete:

Plate 21

60

109

Vixi diu werlt alle min von deme mere unze an den rin
                          dux chünegin.
des wole ih mih darben daz chunich von engellant lege an mi
nen armen.   Item   47.

Soclus flore uario uestitur z ueris presentia
sentitur: phylomena dulcatur modicias auditur.

sic hyemis seuicia finitur. Rubet egne coma uirgre
grata frontem cedit parum inclinata, tota ridet facies fe
lix z beata que tantis est uirtutibz ornata. Vincitur sub an
gulo demore ista uincat balsamum odore, felix qui cum
uirgine struitur sopore, hic dus adequabitur honore.

Distant sup. gytra decentr z equali spacio ridenti os iuuante
osculum simile poscenti subuenti mi domina cadenti

Vuineratus nequeo sanari. nulla uite poterit spet dare
nisi me presceueres uelis consolari. que auncta uincis for
ma speciali. Nah eget sine einen von mir sunne. min

hohgemüeten chuniginne chunne ir daz min steter müt
                                         leibe
vn min herze brinne nah um süze liebe. vn nah ir min.

SL. demore, cum honore.   Item. Item.

Slece uiuerem, nec meroris, nec doloris, ubi tum
legere salutarem gramina me nouarem, nun
do darem noua carmina. Tamen cano z deus no sta
tu ueneris anius paris z scolaris sum cum ethereis